How Loud Can You BURP?

Glenn Murphy received his masters in science communication from London's Imperial College of Science, Technology and Medicine. He wrote his first popular science book, *Why Is Snot Green?*, while in London. In 2007 he moved to the United States. He now lives and works in Raleigh, North Carolina, with his wife, Heather, and an increasingly large and ill-tempered cat.

Why Is Snot Green? was shortlisted for the Blue Peter Book Awards 2007, Best Book with Facts category, and the Royal Society Prizes for Science Books Junior Prize 2008.

Also published by Macmillan
in association with the Science Museum

WHY IS SNOT GREEN?
AND OTHER EXTREMELY IMPORTANT QUESTIONS
(AND ANSWERS) FROM THE SCIENCE MUSEUM
Glenn Murphy

STUFF THAT SCARES YOUR PANTS OFF!
THE SCIENCE MUSEUM BOOK OF SCARY
THINGS (AND WAYS TO AVOID THEM)
Glenn Murphy

SCIENCE SORTED!
EVOLUTION, NATURE AND STUFF
Glenn Murphy

SCIENCE SORTED!
SPACE, BLACK HOLES AND STUFF
Glenn Murphy

WOW: INVENTIONS THAT CHANGED THE WORLD
Philip Ardagh

DO TRY THIS AT HOME!
Punk Science

How Loud Can You BURP?

and other extremely important questions
(and answers) from the Science Museum

Glenn Murphy

Illustrated by Mike Phillips

MACMILLAN CHILDREN'S BOOKS

First published 2008 by Macmillan Children's Books

This edition published 2012 by Macmillan Children's Books
a division of Macmillan Publishers Limited
20 New Wharf Road, London N1 9RR
Basingstoke and Oxford
Associated companies throughout the world
www.panmacmillan.com

ISBN 978-1-4472-2629-1

3 5 7 9 8 6 4 2

A CIP catalogue record for this book is available from
the British Library.

Typeset by Perfect Bound Ltd
Printed and bound in the UK by CPI Group (UK) Ltd, Croydon, CR0 4YY

Contents

To Mum and Dad – this one's for you, folks

Thanks to:

Deborah Bloxam, Damon McCollin-Moore and Gaby Morgan – for their encouragement, their tireless editing and that whole getting-me-to-write-stuff thing

Fran Bate, Emily Scott-Dearing, Dr Peter Morris, Doug Millard, Dan Albert, Alice Nicholls, Katie Maggs, Andrew Nahum, Tilly Blyth, Ben Russell and everyone else at the Science Museum and the NRM who offered their support and comments

Dr Dave Reay at Edinburgh University

Nina Davies and Professor Alun Williams at the Royal Veterinary College

The SCONCs (Science Communicators of North Carolina) – thanks for the hearty welcome

The Witts, the Murphs, the Grosses and the Soareses – especially Ben, Eric and Milo. It's a big world out there, lads – now get exploring.

Introduction

This is a book about questions. Your questions. And, believe me, I've heard a lot of them.

A little while ago, I wrote another book called *Why Is Snot Green?* That was about unanswered questions too. Maybe you read it. If not, you can always rush out and buy it later today. Hint, hint.

Anyway – the Snot-book questions came from visitors to the Science Museum, young and old.

Of course, I couldn't answer them all in just one go. But lots of people liked that little book. So we thought it would be a good idea to write another one. This one.

But this time I wanted more people's questions. I mean, not everybody can come to London and visit the Science Museum just so they can ask, right? So my mate Daniel came up with an idea.

'Why don't we make a web page?' he said. 'Then kids and adults from all over the country – all over the world, even – can read bits of your book and offer their own science-y questions.'

So that's what we did. And we got lots of questions. Hundreds of them. Some of these questions I'd already answered in the first book. And, of course, if you write a book called *Why Is Snot Green?* and ask for

1

more questions for a sequel . . . a whole lot of people are going to give you something like this:

> You got a question from:
> **Name:** Toby
> **Question:** Why is poo brown?
>
> You got a question from:
> **Name:** Jessica
> **Question:** Why is pee yellow?

But, aside from that, you were a creative bunch, and you asked me all sorts of things. Things about your bodies and brains. About the biggest, the smallest and the fastest things in the world. You asked what planes, trains and cars might look like in the future. Lots of you seemed worried about the climate and what will happen to it. And, of course, there were a good number of you who thought: Great! Glenn can do my homework for me! Some of you were more obvious about this than others:

> You got a question from:
> **Name:** Clark
> **Question:** Will Glenn do my science project for me, it's on the universe and black holes thank you very much i expect 'A' quality work. Just send it in an email so i can print it. Pictures give extra credit so yeah add some thanks.

To all you homework-blaggers out there, I say this: YOU'RE 'AVIN' A LAUGH, AIN'TCHA? DO IT YERSELF!!

To everyone else that sent me a question – whether it made it into the book or not – I thank you. And I dedicate this book to you. Hope you like it.

Now let's get cracking . . .

Science of Me

From sunburn to snot, from breathing to burping, few of us ever stop wondering about how our bodies work and what makes us tick. Sure, we study bits of the body at school, and learn all about where our kidneys are, what our lungs do and stuff like that. But what about goosebumps, hiccups and hayfever? Why do we have eyelids but not earlids or noselids?

And what is that thing that dangles down the back of your throat called?*

This chapter is, quite literally, all about you. And you guys weren't short of questions about you, let me tell ya. Some, of course, were easier to answer than others:

> You got a question from:
> **Name:** James
> **Question:** What would happen if you ate poo?

You'd almost certainly throw up, James. Unless you actually *like* eating poo, that is.**

And now, on to the rest . . .

---

* It's called a uvula. It stops food going up your nose and down your windpipe when you swallow.

** Seriously, I wouldn't try it. One gram of faeces contains around 10 million viruses, 1 million bacteria, plus parasite eggs and cysts. Eating poo can make you very ill indeed.

How loud can you burp?

The loudest burp on record is around 105 decibels – louder than a motorbike or chainsaw, and loud enough to cause real pain to anyone close enough to it. But don't try these at home, as they could be dangerous!

Louder than a motorbike?! No way!

Yup. The world-record burp measured 104.9 decibels (decibels, or dB for short, are the units used to measure volume). And that was from over 2.5m away! Close up, the World Champion burper claims to be able to reach 118dB or more. The average motorbike roars away at around 90dB – a full twenty-eight units lower!

So who did it?

An English guy called Paul Hunn. He smashed the previous burping record in July 2004, and no one has topped it yet.

How could he burp so loud?

Well, like all sounds, burps are just waves of air pressure, and, if you make these waves big enough, any sound can become loud. To create a sound, an object – like a bell or guitar string – is made to vibrate back and forth very fast by striking it, plucking it or rubbing something against it. In turn, the object compresses the air molecules around it, making waves or vibrations that are carried through the air. When they reach your ears, these pressure waves vibrate your eardrums. From there, the vibrations are amplified by a set of little bones, picked up by a set of tiny hairs in your cochlea (which is a long, thin tube filled with

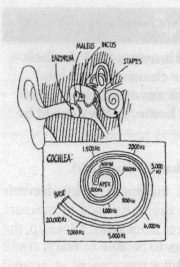

fluid and lined with hairs – all coiled up like a snail shell in your inner ear). Here the vibrations are finally translated into nerve signals that your brain interprets as sounds, such as 'bell', 'guitar string' or whatever.

But what about burps?

In the case of burps, the vibrating object is a fleshy flap called the cardia, which closes off the stomach from the food-tube, or oesophagus. When air is swallowed (either by accident while you're eating, or on purpose if you're trying to force a burp), it gets trapped in the stomach. As the stomach fills with food, liquid and gas, the pressure builds up and the air bursts through the flap – vibrating it on the way out and creating that deep, satisfying BRRRRRRRRRRRRRRPPPPP sound as it goes. Of course, if you want to *force* the burp out, you can squeeze your stomach by contracting your stomach muscles and diaphragm (which is the flat sheet of muscle underneath your stomach and lungs). This is how Mr Hunn made his burp so loud. Millions of kids around the world use the same method to force loud burps. He's just much better at it than anyone else. Oh, and he also swallowed lots of fizzy drink first.

Yeah — why *do* fizzy drinks make you burp like that?

They're made bubbly and fizzy by adding carbon dioxide gas under pressure. So when you drink the drink, you swallow the gas. The gas builds up in your stomach, annnnd . . . you can figure out the rest.

Is it dangerous to make yourself burp like that?

Well, drinking lots of fizzy drinks isn't very good for you, and swallowing air on purpose won't do your stomach any good, but that's not really what makes burping as loud as Mr Hunn does dangerous. It's after the burp leaves the body that it becomes a danger to you and others.

But if a burp is just air and sound, how could it be dangerous to anyone?

If they're loud enough and at the right frequency, sounds can be very powerful and dangerous. Ever hear of opera singers who can shatter glass with their voices alone? Well, that's true. All they have to do is hit the right pitch, and sing the note loud enough, and the glass will vibrate and shake itself to pieces. And the US military have even developed a 'sound weapon' that fires waves of air

pressure and sound instead of bullets. The Vortex Ring Gun shoots a ring of vibrating air that can knock down a grown man over 10m away.

So if you burped loud enough, could you crack a person's glasses? Or knock a bunch of people over? That'd be sweet!

Err . . . no. Not quite. Even the most accomplished burper, like Mr Hunn, couldn't produce enough air pressure to knock someone down. And his burps are too low-pitched to crack glass. But he could burp loud enough to hurt your ears, or even damage them permanently.

What, really?

Yup – really. Mr Hunn burps at between 105 and 118 decibels. 85 decibels is enough to temporarily damage your hearing. Builders using pneumatic drills (which thump away at around 120dB) wear ear defenders to avoid getting hearing damage. If you burped at 165dB, that would be the same as a gunshot going off right next to your head. So burp this loud and you could deafen yourself and other people!

Yeah, and what a let-down too.

Why's that?

Just think — you can burp as loud as a gunshot, but after the first time no one can hear it. Not even you.

Err . . . yeah . . . that'd be a real tragedy.

Just one more thing . . .

What's that?

Do Brussels sprouts make you burp?

I don't . . . think so, no. Why do you ask?

They should do. Cos they come from Belch'um.

Oh *man*, that was bad.

Heh, heh.
BUUUURRRRRRRRRRRRPPPPPPPPPP!!!!

Sci-facts: noisy stuff

The volume of a sound wave is related to its air pressure, and measured in decibels (dB). On the decibel scale, zero decibels marks the softest sound most people can hear (although some people can hear sounds at –10dB or lower). Here's how some common (and uncommon) noises measure up:

dB	Sound
0	rustling leaves
20	whisper
40	light rainfall
75	washing machine
90	motorbike
110	chainsaw, rock concert
115	one of Paul Hunn's burps (at close range)
130	jet aeroplane (from 30m away)
165	shotgun

Why do we get hiccups, and how do you stop them?

Hiccups are a funny one. We know what they are, we know what they do to our bodies and, for the most part, we know how to get rid of them. But we can't say for sure where they come from, or what they actually do in the body.

What is a hiccup, anyway?

A hiccup – or *singultus*, as medical scientists call it – is a kind of forced intake of breath, caused by muscle spasms in your chest and throat. There are over a hundred causes of hiccups, but the most common is irritation of the stomach or the oesophagus – the food tube that leads to the stomach. The 'hic' noise comes when the breath is cut off by the snapping shut of your *glottis* – which is like a fleshy lid or trapdoor that separates the food and air tubes in your throat.

So why are they called hiccups, rather than singultus-es or something?

Good question. That's because the word 'hiccup' is an example of onomatopoeia – a word that sounds like the thing it describes. So hiccups were named after the noise they make.

They weren't always called hiccups. In sixteenth–century English they were called *hickops*. By the seventeenth century they'd become *hiccoughs*, and by the eighteenth they were known as *hickets* or *hyckocks*. The 'hic' part seems pretty universal, as foreign words for hiccup sound similar. The French get *hoquets* and the

Japanese get *hyakkari*. The Germans suffer with the much wetter-sounding *schluckaufs*. Still – it's nice to know that everyone gets them, whatever they're called.

So if everyone gets them, what are they for, exactly?

The truth is, we're not really sure what they're for. According to some scientists, hiccups don't really do anything – they have no function in the body at all (other than to make us look daft). Instead, they think hiccups might be a kind of malfunction in the nerves that control the breathing muscles and glottis, which happens when the nerves get irritated or damaged.

Hiccups are useless, then?

Maybe, but then again maybe not. It could be that they're useless to us *now*, but they once served a purpose in the animals we evolved from. Another idea is that the hiccup evolved to help our four-legged ancestors to swallow food that got stuck in their throats. Where we humans have the luxury of gravity helping food down, quadrupeds (animals that walk on all fours) have to shift their food horizontally to get it from their mouths to their stomachs. This means it's easier for lumps of food to get stuck in their throats. Some scientists think that lumps lodged like this might press down on a nerve in the throat that triggers the hiccup. The sharp breath in then creates a vaccuum behind the food, and helps the animal suck down the lump. This might explain why dogs (not known for eating their food slowly) seem so prone to hiccups – they 'wolf' their food down in big lumps that they have to clear by hiccupping.

Fair enough. But why don't hiccups stop once you stop eating, then?

Well, sometimes they do, and sometimes they don't. Most cases of the hiccups are cured (or go away by themselves) inside a few minutes. Others can go on for weeks, or even years. In fact, doctors give names to different classes of hiccups, depending on how long they go on for. *Common hiccups* are gone within an hour. *Persistent hiccups* can go on for up to forty-eight hours, but are usually harmless (although very annoying!). *Acute hiccups* go on for more than forty-eight hours, and are usually caused by drugs, but they can also occur naturally. For example, in January 2007, a teenager from Florida named Jennifer Mee hiccupped for five weeks straight, for no known reason! If hiccups go on for longer than two months, they're classed as *intractable* or *diabolic hiccups*, and they're usually the sign of a serious illness.

Two months?! That sounds like a nightmare! Is that the longest they can go on for?

Well, the world record stands at 68 years, with a guy called Charles Osbourne (again, from the USA), who hiccupped continuously from 1922 to 1990. The poor guy basically had hiccups for life.

Right — I have to know. How do you get rid of hiccups, really? I heard that if you stand on your head and drink a glass of water . . . no, wait — you have to eat a raw chili pepper, right?

For common hiccups, there are literally hundreds of recommended 'cures' out there. Some involve eating or drinking things, others tell you to hold your breath. Some tell you to drink a glass of water in a certain way, others to get a friend to distract you. In reality, the ones that actually work (and many don't) do so by helping you get control of your breathing. So it doesn't really matter what you eat, or how you drink the water – it's just the interruption of your breathing pattern that does the trick. Holding your breath usually works best, since it's the most direct way of controlling your breathing muscles.

What about getting a friend to scare you?

That usually only works if the hiccups are *psychosomatic* – when you're setting off the jerky contraction in the breathing muscles yourself, but you're not aware that you're doing it. Kind of like imagining each hiccup into existence. It's not always easy to tell when this is happening, but getting someone to distract you can snap you out of it long enough for them to stop. Of course, none of these remedies is likely to work on acute or intractable hiccups. As they're usually started by drugs or nerve damage, they're often only treatable with more drugs. That said, some researchers have claimed success treating hiccups with needles, radiation or even digital rectal massage.

What's that, then?

A finger up the bum.

What?! I think I'd rather have hiccups!

Maybe so.

Top 10 weird hiccup cures (that may or may not work)

1   Breathe in and hold it until they're gone.
2   Eat a spoonful of mustard.
3   Eat a raw chili pepper.
4   Immerse your face in ice water.
5   Stand on your head.
6   Rub your earlobe.
7   Start running. Stop when the hiccups do.
8   Take off your left sock and breathe through it for one minute.
9   Tell yourself 'I haven't got the hiccups', 50 times.
10 Do nothing – just wait for the next hiccup. Repeat until it doesn't come.

Why do we breathe, and why do we need lungs to do it?

We breathe to capture oxygen, which helps us convert food into energy in our cells, and to get rid of carbon dioxide – the waste gas that is formed as this happens. Our lungs pump these gases in and out of our bodies, and help us dissolve them in and out of our blood.

So let me get this straight — we breathe so that our cells can eat food?

Not exactly, but close. It's more like 'we breathe so that our cells can breathe, and eat so that our cells can eat'.

What? They *breathe* too? Now I'm really confused . . .

OK, let's go back a bit. If you think about it, cells are like little units of life. The smallest living things, bacteria, are just individual cells swimming about eating stuff. They absorb sugars or other nutrients from the air or liquid around them, and turn this 'food' into energy – which they can use to grow, multiply and squidge around looking for more food.

Got that.

OK. Now some of these bacteria eventually evolved into bigger creatures like fish, frogs, lizards, monkeys and human beings. Those particular types of bacteria are called aerobic bacteria, which means . . .

. . . that they wore tracksuits and did lots of exercise?

Err . . . no. It means they have to 'breathe' (or take in) oxygen in order to turn their food into energy.

Oh yeah, of course. I knew that. I mean, nobody makes tracksuits that small, for starters.

Err . . . right. Anyway, these bacteria and the animal cells they evolved into all need to take in oxygen for that same reason – to fuel their food-processors and produce usable energy.

But why do they need oxygen to do that? Couldn't they do it without oxygen?

Well, they can for a while, at least. But the main power source for aerobic bacteria and cells comes from a chain reaction which uses oxygen – so they can't survive without it for long. Oxygen and nutrients go into this reaction, then energy and carbon dioxide come out. The energy is stored and moved around in special molecules, while the carbon dioxide has to be removed from the cell, as it forms an acid if too much of it builds up. So, in a way, aerobic

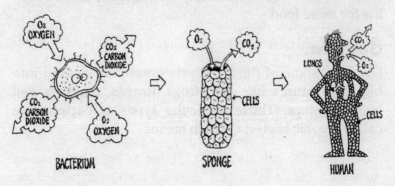

bacteria 'breathe in' oxygen and 'breathe out' carbon dioxide. These bacteria evolved into complex animals by clustering together and eventually developing into the cells, tissues, organs and systems that make whole animal bodies. But, since each cell still needs nutrients and oxygen for energy, the whole animal has to keep eating and breathing just to supply them.

OK — that kind of makes sense. But why do bigger animals need lungs to breathe?

Well, if you think about it, the bigger an animal gets, the more cells it has, and the further away from the air its insides are. Up to a certain size, animals can absorb oxygen through their skin and let it spread through their tissues. But most things bigger than flatworms need air tubes of some kind to get air to the inner parts of the body (that works for insects and spiders, at least). For larger, more complex or more active animals, you need some kind of gas-exchanging air pump. That's where lungs come in.

But not all animals have lungs, right? I mean, fish don't, do they?

Right – they don't. Fish have gills instead. They swallow water and use their gills to absorb the oxygen dissolved in it. Then the gills dump carbon dioxide back into the water before pushing it out. That's what's happening when you see the gills 'flapping' on a fish.

So why can't we just swallow oxygen and burp out the carbon dioxide?

Well, then you'd be swallowing continuously, every few seconds, all day long. Like a big, walking air-fish. Not much fun, and kind of tricky to hold down

conversations. Plus it wouldn't work anyway, since swallowed air goes to your stomach – which is already specialized for digesting food, and is too small for exchanging breathing gases.

Why does size matter?

You need a large surface area for the gas exchange to happen quickly enough between the air you take in and your bloodstream, which carries it to cells throughout the body. That's where lungs come in handy. They're more than just air sacks – they're like giant air sponges which soak up and exchange gases very quickly through thousands of tiny bobbles, called alveoli.

You're telling me I have pasta in my lungs?

No. That's ravioli.

Oh. I knew that.

Alveoli are the clustered, berry-like bobbles found at the end of the branching air tubes deep in your lungs. They help increase the surface area of your lungs so much that if you flattened them all out into one sheet, it'd cover about 75 square metres – roughly the size of a tennis court. When you breathe in, muscles around and beneath the lungs help them suck air into the alveoli. These are covered in tiny blood vessels so that oxygen can move into the bloodstream and be carried around the body. Carbon dioxide gas moves the other way – the bloodstream carries it out of organs and tissues and back to the air inside the alveoli, ready to be pumped out again as you breathe out. And there you have it – you and all your cells have all the oxygen they need, provided you keep breathing air, and avoid damaging all your delicate breathing equipment with dangerous fumes or cigarette smoke.

Got it. Don't breathe cigarette smoke — or pasta — and your cells can keep doing aerobics.

Something like that.

Sci-Facts: lungs and stuff

The animal with the *largest lungs on Earth* is the **blue whale**, which may also be the largest animal ever to have lived. At up to 30m long and 135 tonnes in weight, the blue whale is even larger than the biggest dinosaurs ever found. A blue whale's lungs hold up to 2,000 litres of air – compared with about four litres for the average human.

Elephant seals and **sperm whales** can hold a single breath for up to two hours! The human world record stands at 15 minutes 2 seconds, achieved by German diver **Tom Sietas** in August 2007.

The lungs are the **largest organs** in the human body (unless you count the skin, which can be thought of as an organ or a tissue). The average male lungs weigh about 1kg, while the average weight for female lungs is 930g. This doesn't explain, however, why boys are usually louder . . .

Why do we have eyelids, but not earlids?

Because eyelids helped us – or rather our animal ancestors – to survive, whereas earlids would've made little difference to whether they survived or not.

How could eyelids help us survive? I mean, what makes *them* so important?

Well, what makes *any* bit of your body important? What about your hands – what good are they?

That's easy — we can use them to pick things up and make things. Use tools and stuff.

Right – and how would that have helped our early human ancestors survive?

They could build shelters. And catch food. And make fires for cooking it.

Spot on. But how many of those things could they have done easily without being able to see?

Err . . . dunno. I guess they could have just about done them. But it would've been much harder. But we're talking about eyelids, not eyes. You can still see without eyelids, can't you?

Yes, you can. But, if you're a land animal, then not for long.

Why not?

Think about it – what are eyelids really for?

Stopping stuff getting in your eyes?

Like what?

Dust. Muck. Shampoo.

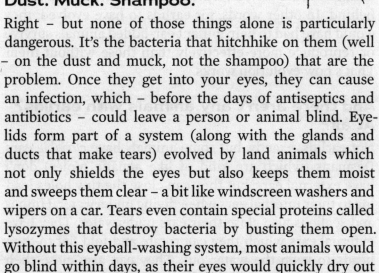

Right – but none of those things alone is particularly dangerous. It's the bacteria that hitchhike on them (well – on the dust and muck, not the shampoo) that are the problem. Once they get into your eyes, they can cause an infection, which – before the days of antiseptics and antibiotics – could leave a person or animal blind. Eyelids form part of a system (along with the glands and ducts that make tears) evolved by land animals which not only shields the eyes but also keeps them moist and sweeps them clear – a bit like windscreen washers and wipers on a car. Tears even contain special proteins called lysozymes that destroy bacteria by busting them open. Without this eyeball-washing system, most animals would go blind within days, as their eyes would quickly dry out and become infected.

So do all animals have eyelids, then?

Not all of them. Most mammals, birds, reptiles and amphibians do, but fish do not – since they don't really need to keep their eyes moist underwater. Animals that evolved to live on land but then later returned to the water (like seals and otters) generally do have eyelids, but some whales do not. They've long since lost them, since they were no longer needed to ward off airborne bacteria. Dolphins, though, do still have eyelids. Maybe because they swim much faster, so need eyelids to help protect their eyes against debris whipping by them in the water.

OK — so eyelids are pretty important. But wouldn't earlids be useful too?

Possibly. But not so useful that without them earlid-less animals would die out, leaving mostly ear-lidded animals behind. In other words, for earlids to have evolved, they would have had to help mutant ear-lidded animals survive or reproduce more effectively than those without them. That's how evolution works.

And there aren't any animals with earlids? At all?

Not earlids, exactly, but some animals have *closable* ears. Desmans (which are kind of like aquatic moles) don't have external ears, but they can close the tiny holes leading to their internal ears when diving underwater. Hippos and sealions also close their ears underwater. They have external ears which they can rotate and fold flat to their heads to keep the water out. They can also close their nostrils – which is a bit like having noselids, I suppose.

Cool! So could we ever evolve earlids and noselids in the future?

It's possible, I guess. But remember – nothing evolves *on purpose*. Evolution works by picking out mutations. Mutations happen by chance, all the time – but most either have no effect on the life form, or are bad for it. *Useful* mutations are quite rare. But it's these that allow organisms to evolve. If a mutation proves useful enough, it'll be passed on to more of the mutant's offspring, and over time it becomes a new feature of the species (since most or all animals of that species will end up with the mutation). So for us to evolve earlids or noselids, there would have to be a) mutant people with earlids and noselids (or at least the beginnings of them); and b) some sort of pressure in our environment that gradually killed off people *without* earlids and noselids, or prevented them from having kids. And it would have to happen over a long period of time, as evolution usually works very slowly – over hundreds, thousands or millions of years, rather than days or months.

What about if global warming made all the oceans flood the land, and we had to live in boats and feed only on sea animals? And we had no fishing rods. So we had to dive for shellfish and stuff all the time. Would that do it?

Well, being able to close your ears and nose might help equalize pressure while you're diving, I guess, but . . .

Excellent. What about flippers and fishtails? And gills so we can breathe underwater?

I'll leave you to figure that out, I think.

Hmmm . . . so first the air gets all poisonous so we can't breathe — no, wait — the surface of the sea freezes over so we can't come up for air, and . . .

Why can't you smell your own farts, when other people can?

Because they're more sensitive to your particular brand of bottom burp than you are. Or you're just refusing to own up to it.

So some people are better fart-sniffers than others?

Well, yes – in a way, I suppose. But it'd be fairer (and more polite) to say that some people are better sniffers than others, generally – not just of farts, but of all kinds of different smells.

Why would that be?

Because people vary in the smell detectors they're born with.

You mean some people have bigger noses than others?

Actually, how big the nose is doesn't have much to do with it. It's more to do with how many special odour-detecting sensors they've got up their nose, and how finely tuned they are to different smells. These special proteins, called chemoreceptors, send signals to the brain when they detect the presence of certain chemicals in the air. Each receptor recognizes the shape of just one type of chemical molecule. When that molecule enters the nose and binds to the correct receptor, it triggers a nerve signal that whizzes to a special region of the brain called the olfactory region ('olfaction' is the scientific name for smelling, so 'olfactory' just means 'used for smelling').

Here, signals from lots of different receptors are decoded, and your brain interprets the result as 'grass', 'chocolate', 'fart' or whatever. How well you can detect smells, and distinguish between similar smells, depends on how many of each different type of receptor you have. This can differ quite a bit between two people, which makes some people far more sensitive to smells (and better able to tell the difference between 'your fart' and 'my fart') than others.

So if you can't smell your own fart, it means you have a worse sense of smell than people around you?

Not necessarily. Other things can affect your ability to interpret smells too. Catching a cold, for example, produces mucus that clogs the inner passages of the nose and stops the odour-carrying air reaching the chemoreceptors so easily. This is why you can't smell anything much with a snotty nose. But even if you have a clear nose and a better sense of smell than those around you, you still might not notice your own 'trouser coughs' before others do.

Why not? I mean, the fart begins at your bottom, right?

Right.

And it spreads out from there?

Correct. The smelly fart gas released from your bottom gradually spreads outwards (or diffuses) to fill the room, reaching closer noses first and more distant noses last. (Unless someone comes to the rescue by opening a window, that is.)

So if *your* nose is closest to your own bottom, how could you not get the first whiff?

Because even though the fart reaches your nose first, you might not recognize it. Or, more accurately, your nose might recognize it, but decide to ignore it.

Why would it do that?

Because of the way your nose, and other sense organs in the body, are designed. Your senses – including sight, hearing, smell, taste and touch – all evolved to detect *changes* to your surroundings or environment, rather than things that stay the same. So if you constantly or repeatedly experience the same sensation – like a continuous sound, smell or touch – then your senses can sometimes 'tune out' this sensation as 'background noise'. That's why when you first put a ring on your finger, you can feel its weight and pressure. But after a while this constant sensation is tuned out by your brain, and you can't feel it (or rather don't take any notice of it) any more. The same thing happens with sounds and smells. You might hear the continuous hum of the new fridge in your kitchen for an hour or so, but after a while you don't hear it at all unless you're trying to. And although the smell of a bad egg or stink bomb seems to quickly go away on its own, it's often still there – but your nose is ignoring it.

. . . so if you're always dropping your own 'bad eggs', then after a while you might not smell them so easily?

Right. If you've been gently farting away all day, then unless this latest 'eggy rumble' is notably stinkier or otherwise different to the last, your nose might happily ignore it as part of your ever present 'background' smell . . . while your friends get the full nasal assault.

Of course, there is a simpler explanation of why you can't smell it and others can.

What's that?

You're lying.

What? No way! Err . . . I mean, how would that work?

Quite simple. You've farted, and it's slightly stinky. But apparently nobody's heard it, and you're hoping they haven't smelt it either. Even if they do, they've got no proof it was you, so you can blame someone or something else (see list of useful scapegoats on page 28).

As *if*. I would *never* do that.

Of course not.

27

Practical science: things to blame a fart on

If it's noisy
A creaky floorboard
A passing motorbike
A neighbour playing the saxophone

If it's stinky
The compost heap in the garden
Sprouts boiling in the kitchen
Eggs rotting in the bin

If it's noisy *and* stinky
The dog
Someone else
Anyone else

If it's neither noisy *nor* stinky
What's the problem? If a fart is neither heard nor smelt, is it really a fart at all? Think about it . . .

Why does pollen give you hayfever?

Because some people's bodies are paranoid and overreact to it. They treat harmless pollen like a dangerous alien invader and launch a full counter-attack that clogs up their eyes and noses.

But why do only some people get it?

Because not everybody (or rather, not everybody's-body!) reacts to pollen this way. Only people who have become extra-sensitive (or *hypersensitive*) to inhaled pollen get the reaction that causes the symptoms of hayfever. They literally become allergic to pollen.

And how does that happen? Are they just born like that?

For some sufferers – yes. Scientists have recently found a gene that may be involved in hayfever and other allergic reactions. If you're born with a certain version of this gene, you may be much more likely to develop hayfever when you grow up. This particular gene helps manage your body's *immune system* – which controls your ability to fight off the bacteria and viruses that cause diseases.

So hayfever is caused by a virus?

No, it isn't. But, in a way, people that have hayfever treat pollen as if it is one.

When you inhale a nasty microbe – a virus or bacterium that could cause disease – your body's self-defence system (or immune system) responds to it in several ways. First, immune cells stick to a few of the microbes, chew them up and leave bits of them (called *antigens*) sticking out for other cells to examine. These antigens are often bits of outer shell or coat from the bacterium or virus.

Next, more immune cells encounter these bits, clone themselves and make thousands of proteins called antibodies. The antibodies recognize the antigens (that's where the name comes from – they're *anti*body *gen*erators) and help launch a massive counter-attack that destroys all remaining microbes of the same type.

Finally, some of the antibodies – and the cells that create them – stick around to ward off future attacks. If the same microbe is inhaled again, these cells and antibodies can launch an even quicker response, and deal with it way before it causes any symptoms of disease. This is why the first time you're infected by something like chickenpox or measles, it causes the nasty symptoms of disease (like spots on the skin, swelling and fever). After that, you're immune, and you don't even notice your body comfortably fighting off further attacks.

I THOUGHT THESE MIGHT CHEER YOU UP!

But what has that got to do with hayfever?

In hayfever sufferers, it's thought that their immune systems respond to pollen as if it was a nasty microbe, because some immune cells in their noses are made hypersensitive to it. Instead of ignoring pollen in the nose as an irritating (but harmless) bit of muck, these cells launch an over-the-top counter-attack. They release a substance called histamine, which helps bring immune cells (as reinforcements) to the area from the blood-stream. Histamine makes the blood vessels swell and leak so that the immune cells can squeeze through the walls to reach the 'deadly' pollen particles. Unfortunately, this also leaves the eyes and nose all red, itchy, watery and clogged with white goo.

Of course, this explains nicely how hayfever happens once you have hypersensitive immune cells. But it doesn't explain how your cells got so pollen-sensitive in the first place. And that one faulty gene alone can't explain *all* the hayfever sufferers out there.

Why's that?

For the last hundred years, the number of hayfever sufferers seems to have been increasing *hugely* in many places around the world, and that one gene probably can't account for them all – there are just too many of them. Since people (especially children) in cities and towns get hayfever far more than people in the countryside, some scientists thought that it might be down to pollution. But pollution alone probably can't explain all the new cases either.

Why not?

Among other things, it wasn't people living in the most polluted areas that developed hayfever fastest. In many towns and cities, hayfever seemed to crop up most among families with fewer children – often those that lived in richer, cleaner areas away from busy roads and factories. That got scientists to thinking that the reason for this sensitivity to pollen might be something else.

Like what?

One theory is that hayfever develops when you encounter too much pollen at once, after never having been exposed to pollen before. So, while people in the countryside breathe in a lot of pollen, they're exposed to it slowly and gradually, and their immune systems become used to it and ignore it. In the cities, some children never encounter pollen in the air until the height of the tree pollination season, when the wind gusts a big cloud of it in from the surrounding countryside. This shocks the immune cells into thinking it's an all-out microbe assault, making them hypersensitive to pollen from then onwards.

So you get hayfever because you're suddenly hit with loads of pollen all at once?

Yup. Could be. This 'all at once' theory seems to explain a few other mysteries too. Such as why there was little or no hayfever in Japan before 1950, but now most Japanese children and adults suffer with it. This was because millions of cedar trees were planted in Japan after World War Two to create timber for building and selling – which exposed millions of Japanese people to huge amounts of cedar pollen for the first time. Since then, the number of cedar trees has stayed the same, but the number of cars on Japanese roads has gone up enormously. So it could be a combination of 'pollen shock' and pollution that has given so many Japanese people hayfever. Add the faulty gene to that mix, and this probably explains the overall increase in hayfever worldwide.

Can you stop it, once you've got it?

If you have hayfever already, there are lots of good medicines that work by blocking the action of histamine and help to stop the eyes and nose from watering and itching. If you don't have hayfever, and you live in a big town or city, it might be a good idea to escape the pollution and build up your 'pollen immunity' by getting out to parks and the countryside as much as you can. Even if it doesn't stop you getting hayfever, it'll be healthier than staying indoors or hanging out near roads – for any number of other reasons. Plus you can learn more outdoors than you can indoors, which will make you a wonderfully intelligent and interesting person. If you don't believe me – weigh this lot up:

Stuff you can become an expert on indoors
PlayStation, Xbox, Wii, music,
whatever you can find on TV or the Internet

Stuff you can become an expert on outdoors
Football, tennis, volleyball, rugby, cricket, hockey,
lacrosse, climbing, hiking, running, cycling,
potholing, skiing, surfing, skating, boarding, kung fu,
karate, t'ai chi, scuba diving, swimming, diving, flora,
fauna, music (with an iPod)

Why do we get goosebumps when we get cold or scared?

It's a reaction left over from our evolutionary past. Our animal ancestors were much hairier than us, and 'goosebumps' helped them
a) stay warmer, and
b) look bigger and scarier.

What have goosebumps got to do with being hairy?

Everything! Goosebumps are quite literally a hair-raising reaction. The scientific name for a goosebump is a piloerection, which just means 'hair standing up' in Latin. And that's exactly what happens. Each hair on the body has a set of tiny muscles beneath it. When stimulated, these tighten up, creating a dent right under the base of the hair, and a raised ring of skin around it. This makes the hair stand up straight. Depending on how hairy you are, you might not have an actual hair follicle on that spot any more (or, if you do, it might be too small or too fair to see). But the muscles are still there under the skin, so when stimulated they will still contract, making a bump (or, more accurately, a raised crater – a bit like a tiny skin-volcano).

Why are they called goosebumps?

Because on hairless skin a whole set of these bumps look a bit like the knobbly skin of a goose (or any other bird, for that matter) after it has been plucked for cooking. Eating geese isn't so common any more, but the name comes from a time when it was, and has stuck around.

So you could rename them chickenbumps, or ostrichbumps?

If it made you feel better, yes. Although 'chickenbumps' sounds a bit too much like chicken pox, which is something else entirely, and 'ostrichbumps' makes them sound like especially large, super-sized goosebumps . . .

Maybe you get them when you're *really* cold, or *properly* scared. Yeah — ostrichbumps . . .

O-kay . . . if you say so. Call 'em what you like.

But how does having your hairs stick up help you stay warm, anyway? Wouldn't that let more cold air on to your skin?

Well, keeping warm is less about 'keeping the cold out' and more about 'keeping the heat in'. When you feel cold, it's actually because you're losing heat from your skin to the colder air around you. If you have a lot of body hair (like our early human-like ancestors and the ape-like animals before them), then raising a whole carpet of hairs traps a layer of warm air next to your skin. This slows down the rate of heat loss from the skin's surface, keeping you warmer. Of course, most humans aren't nearly hairy enough for this to have much of an effect now, so the hair-raising reaction is quite useless. Instead, we wear clothes next to our skin, and the clothing fibres help trap warm air and slow heat loss instead.

So, if we'd never started wearing clothes, we'd still be mega-hairy all over?

Well, not mega-hairy, but *hairier* maybe. Our ancestors

didn't start making or wearing clothes until they'd lost much of their body hair already. It was probably making fires and building shelters to keep warm that reduced the need for a thick coat of all-over body hair in early humans. Plus there are many places in the world (such as parts of the tropics, and some regions near the equator) where it stays fairly warm all the time. People from those regions tend to wear fewer clothes and have far less body hair than those from, say, northern Europe or Asia. So we may have gradually lost our body hair even without clothes.

OK, so for a while goosebumps helped us to keep warm . . . but why do you get them at other times, like when you're scared or excited?

Again, we haven't got enough hair now for this to make any difference, but for our hairy animal ancestors the hair-raising reaction made them look bigger and scarier. If you've ever seen a startled cat, you'll have seen this in action. When surprised or alarmed by another animal, a

cat arches its back, stretches up to stand as tall as it can and its fur stands on end. This makes the cat look quite a bit bigger than it really is, making the other animal think twice about attacking it. Lots of hairy animals use a similar tactic, including apes like gorillas and chimpanzees, which are not too different from the animals we evolved from. Now, of course, this reaction is no use to us at all. But that doesn't stop goosebumps from happening when we're scared or afraid. Even if we're just watching a creepy movie.

But sometimes you get them when you're not scared at all — just excited or nervous. What's up with that?

That's because the hair-raising reaction can happen in two different ways. When you're cold, your nervous system senses the temperature and sends signals to each hair follicle, telling the muscles beneath them to contract as an automatic reflex. But when you're scared, excited or emotional, something else happens. A hormone (or chemical signal carried through the bloodstream) called adrenalin is released from a pair of glands that sit on top of your kidneys. This affects your body in a number of ways that prepares it to do battle or run away (it's sometimes called a 'fight or flight' reaction, for that reason). This includes speeding up your heart rate, increasing blood flow to your muscles and triggering the hair-raising muscles in an attempt to make you look big and scary.

Cool! I've got to try this out. I'm off to startle the cat.

Well, if you want to see your own reaction, you'll need someone to startle *you*.

What do you m—

BOO!!

Yaaaaggghhhhh!!

Heh, heh.

That wasn't funny. I nearly — oh, wait — goosebumps!

Told ya.

Why do spicy things taste hot, even when they're cold?

Because the family of protein sensors that detect hot and cold things on your skin and tongue can also be triggered by chemicals found in spicy things.

Hold on — you've lost me there. What's a protein sensor when it's at home?

It's a clever biological molecule that changes shape when it's activated by a specific chemical or by a temperature change. This starts a chain reaction that sends a nerve signal to your brain, telling it the chemical (or temperature change) has been detected. So it acts like a chemical or temperature sensor.

How does protein do all that? I thought protein was just something you ate to help you grow and make you strong and brainy.

Well, it is. But did you ever think about why? Or, for that matter, why you need to eat food at all?

For energy?

That's part of it. But it's also to build structures and biological machinery within your body. Different foods are needed for different purposes, and you need a good balance of all of them to stay healthy. The three major types of food molecule are carbohydrates, fats and proteins. Carbohydrates is the name given to sugars and starches. (Starches are found in 'starchy' foods like potatoes and pasta.) Carbohydrates are mostly used as an energy source – powering your brain, muscles and pretty much every type of tissue in your body – but they also form structural frameworks within and between cells. Fats are used to build walls (or *membranes*) around cells in your body, for insulation to keep you warm and as cushioning around your organs to keep them safe. Fats are also used as a slow-burning energy source – kept in reserve and used when your blood sugar dips too low. So carbohydrates and fats are very important as building materials and fuels, but they're fairly simple and can't do much beyond that. Proteins, however, come in an incredible variety of different shapes and sizes, folding themselves into highly complex structures to perform a wide range of functions. It's proteins that do all the really clever stuff in the body.

Like what?

Some build things by joining other molecules together.

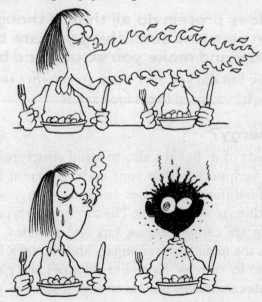

Others destroy things by breaking them apart. Haemo-globin proteins carry oxygen from the lungs to the rest of your body. Antibody proteins attack bacteria and viruses, surrounding them or punching holes in them. Transcription proteins read your DNA, and translation proteins decode it – directing the construction of every last cell in your body, and controlling every function that takes place in them. And sensory proteins detect changes both inside and outside your body – relaying all kinds of information to your brain. This includes information about body temperature, blood pressure, the contents of your blood, the contents of the air around you, light, sound, colour, smells, tastes and more.*

Whoa! So pretty clever little things, then?

I'd say so, yes! Plus some protein families have evolved to do more than one type of job. Like the sensory proteins inside the nerve endings under your skin. One family of these, called 'the TRP channels', is used to sense extreme temperature changes on your skin – like when freezing ice or boiling water come into contact with it. But they're also used for vision, smell and other purposes.

Like for tasting spicy things?

Well, they didn't really evolve *for* that – it just so happens that they're triggered, accidentally, by some spicy things. Or, rather, they react to chemicals (or compounds) found in the leaves and seeds of certain plants. Each type of TRP-channel protein senses a different range of temperatures. One called TRP-A1 detects temperatures from 10–15 °C, which is cold enough to cause pain. Another,

---

* For more about how proteins help your eyes to detect colours, see *Do all people see the same colours?* (page 180).

called TRP-M8, senses the 20–25 °C range, and yet another (TRP-V1) senses temperatures between 40 and 45 °C. But these proteins also react to plant compounds, sending the same signal to your brain as if they had been heated up or cooled down. So the plant things make the proteins send false 'hot' and 'cold' signals to the brain.

The capsaicin compound in chilis triggers the TRP-V1 protein, simulating heat, while the menthol compound in mint triggers the TRP-M8 protein, simulating cold. The effect is worst in sensitive areas with lots of nerve endings (and lots of TRP channels), like on the lips and tongue and around the eyes. That's why chilis burn your tongue, while mint makes it feel cold. Other plant compounds found in garlic, horseradish and mustard affect TRP proteins too, causing 'false hot' or 'false cold' effects in a similar way.

But why would plants make chemicals that make our lips burn or our tongues freeze? Are they trying to hurt us?

Not hurt us, but put us off eating them, maybe. It could be that some plants evolved to produce these 'spicy' compounds to put small mammals off eating them, leaving them to be scoffed by birds instead. Birds don't seem sensitive to spicy foods (perhaps because they have a different set of TRP proteins), so spicy plants may be using a sort of chemical weapon which fights off mammals but avoids deterring birds.

But why would a plant want a bird to eat it instead of a mammal?

Because some plants spread their seeds by getting animals to eat them, carry them around in their stomachs, and eventually – ahem – plant them ...

You mean, poo them out?

Yes – thank you . . . some distance away. And since birds fly further than most mammals can walk or scurry, a plant can spread itself over a wider distance via bird than it would via mammal. Spicy plants couldn't have done this on purpose, of course. But once a few of them had started producing mammal-repelling 'spicy' compounds, those plants spread further (and so survived better) than those without them. Later the 'non-spicy' ones died off, leaving only the 'spicy' plants behind. And bingo – a new spicy species had evolved.

So why do we eat spices if they're supposed to put us off?

Partly because in small amounts, we can enjoy the tingly 'hot' or 'cold' sensations spices bring to our food, and partly because we get less sensitive to them the more we eat them. If we eat enough, the TRP channels stop firing altogether. When this happens, the TRP sensor proteins not only stop reacting to the spice, but they also stop reacting to temperature, pressure or pain. That's why people who eat spicy food a lot can generally handle the hottest spices. And it's also why your mouth goes numb after eating a very spicy curry, or after using very minty toothpaste or mouthwash. The numbing sensation is so strong, in fact, that chili, garlic and mint extracts are used in some traditional or natural medicines as painkillers.

You mean rubbing chili or mint into a sore spot to make it go numb? Yowch! No, thanks!

Hey – don't knock it till you've tried it. I used mint choc chip ice cream for a stubbed toe yesterday, and that worked.

You mean you put your toe in a tub of ice cream?!

No – I ate it all. But I do feel better . . .

Top 10 spicy peppers

The spiciness of peppers is measured using 'heat' units called Scoville units. Here's how some common peppers measure up.

Type of pepper	Scoville units	Common effect
Bell (green or red)	0	none
Sweet Italian	0	smiling
Italian pepperoncini	500	munching happily
Mexican poblano	1,500	drooling
Jalapeno	5,000	sweating
Serrano	23,000	heavy breathing
Cayenne	50,000	asking for water
Thai (red or green)	100,000	flapping tongue in air
Jamaican Scotch bonnet	250,000	screaming
Habanero (Mexico/Caribbean)	300,000	calling the fire brigade

Why does the sun darken your skin but lighten your hair?

Because sunlight does different things to both. It damages skin cells – so your skin darkens to protect itself – but it also stops new hairs from darkening as they grow.

Sunlight damages your skin? What are we, vampires or something? I thought getting out in the sunshine was supposed to be good for you . . .

It is. But, like most things, too much of it can be bad for you too.

But we need sunlight to live, don't we?

That's true, we do. You, me and pretty much every living thing on the planet depend on the Sun's rays for energy. The Sun warms the Earth, its atmosphere and its oceans, keeping the whole lot warm enough for animals, plants, fungi and micro-organisms to survive. Plants and bacteria use sunlight to grow, forming an energy source for all the other living things that feed on them. And even things that live their whole lives cut off from sunlight – in deep ocean trenches, or deep underground – feed on other things that couldn't exist without the warmth and energy provided by the Sun. In humans, sunlight is particularly important, as it helps us make vitamin D in our skin, helps us keep our sleep cycles* regular, and even keeps us happy – by triggering the release of 'happy chemicals' called *endorphins* in our brains.

---

* For more about sleep and why we need it, see *Why do we need sleep?* (page 197).

There you go, then. It's good stuff. We need it.

Yup – we sure do. But we also need food, water and oxygen – and those can be bad for you too. In fact, too much of any one of them could kill you.

What?! No way!

It's true. Too much food can make you obese, which causes heart disease, diabetes and other problems. Too much water can kill you through hyper-hydration, which is the no-less-deadly opposite of dehydration. And too much oxygen can kill you through oxygen toxicity – as, believe it or not, high concentrations of oxygen can damage your cells. (And, if you're wondering why this doesn't happen all the time, it's because the air you breathe is only 21% oxygen – most of the rest of it being nitrogen – so this isn't usually a problem.) Just because something is good for you in small doses doesn't mean *more* of it is *even better* for you. And, for many of us, that's how it is with sunlight.

So what does sunlight do to your skin?

That depends on your skin type, how long it's exposed to the sun and whether or not you've used sunscreen. Unless you're lucky enough to have naturally dark skin (and even dark skin can be damaged if exposed for long enough), then the ultraviolet radiation within sunlight penetrates your skin cells and damages the DNA inside them.

Yikes!

Thankfully, though, your cells contain a kind of biological DNA-repair machine made out of a group of proteins, which usually notices and fixes the damage soon after it's done.*

Phew!

But if your skin-cell DNA sustains too much damage too quickly – through too much exposure to sunlight – then your repair proteins can't keep up. So your skin cells react by darkening themselves, which they do by producing more of a dark pigment protein called melanin. This partly shields the cells, helping to prevent further damage to the DNA, and buying a little time for the existing damage to repair itself.

So suntans are good, then. They stop your skin getting damaged by the sun, right?

Unfortunately, no. A suntan is evidence of skin damage, not healthy skin. A light tan that gradually fades is fine. But, unless you're naturally dark-skinned, a constant, dark tan (the kind people sometimes try to keep up using sunbeds) is a sign of constant, ongoing skin damage. If you get sunburned on the route to tanning, then at worst you could eventually develop skin cancer. At best, keeping an unnaturally dark tan will make your skin age more quickly – making it drier, less stretchy and more wrinkly.

What about your hair? Is too much sun bad for that too?

Not really, since sunlight has a different effect on hair than it does on skin – although it also involves the dark melanin protein that gives you a suntan.

---

* For more about proteins and the clever stuff they do in the body, see *Do all people see the same colours?* (page 180).

But wouldn't that make your hair go darker in the sun? That's not what happens at all.

Right. Over time, some (but not all) types of hair seem to get lightened or bleached by the sun. But when this happens, the hair actually starts out light, and just fails to get darker as it grows.

Eh?

Well, as you probably know, hair grows from the roots, rather than the ends. It's made of long threads of a protein called keratin, which are made by hair cells in your scalp (and elsewhere). These threads are then bundled together into fibres, which start out a bit like soft, transparent rope. Melanin – the 'darkening' protein – is added to these soft fibres at the root of each hair follicle, and the newly grown hair is then pushed out into the sunshine. When sunlight hits the hair, the keratin hardens, and you're left with a dark hair (or a non-white one, at least – without the melanin, that's what colour it would be).

So what difference does more sunshine make?

More or stronger sunlight causes the keratin to harden more quickly, which stops the melanin binding to it so easily. Hence, more sun means less melanin in each hair, and the less melanin you have, the more blonde the hair becomes. This is also why sun-bleached hair darkens again once you're back to 'regular' amounts of sunlight – the soft fibres growing from the root start binding melanin once more, and the blonde hairs 'grow out'. (This is also why dark hair bleached with chemicals quickly becomes dark at the roots too – unless you keep on bleaching the roots, the hair there keeps growing the way it always did, ignoring the lighter hair above.)

So sunlight isn't bad for your hair, it just changes its colour for a bit?

Right. Although you can still get sunburned on your scalp *through* hair, which is why wearing a hat is a good idea if you're out in the sun all day.

OK, then — if some sun is good for you, but too much is bad for you . . . what are you supposed to do?

Get out in it, but be prepared. If you have fair skin, you can cover up and use sunscreen to prevent getting burned. But if you spend *all* day covered up, you're not getting the benefits of the sun on your skin either (like making vitamin D in your skin). So the best way is to get a little sun on your skin, but cover up or duck into the shade way before you start to burn. Just ten minutes in direct sunlight is enough to boost your vitamin D levels. How long it takes for you to burn is down to your own skin type, and how sunny it is where you are. My pale, freckly skin starts to burn after about thirty minutes in the summer sun. If I'm daft enough to lie in it for an hour, I look like a lobster. For you, it may be different.

So 'catching a few rays' = good, 'lobster tan' = bad.

Spot on. Just wish I'd learned that a bit earlier. Yowch!

Top 10 worst places to get sunburned (from pasty Glenn's own experience)

1 Face
2 Back
3 Shoulders
4 Chest
5 Stomach
6 Thighs
7 Feet
8 Behind the knees
9 In the armpits
10 Greece

Because hair-colour genes are passed down from parents to children in different combinations, giving a range of possible colours – including red.

What have genes got to do with it?

Genes have something to do with pretty much everything that happens in our body. Some features, like hair and eye colour, are controlled almost completely by genes. Other things, like height, weight and even intelligence, are partly controlled by genes, and partly by what you *do* with your body (like how much you eat, exercise and learn) as you grow and develop.

But why? What makes genes so important, and how do they work?

Well, that's kind of a long story – but here's the short version. Well – short-ish . . .

Every cell in your body has a bit in the middle that contains DNA. This is the stuff that genes are made of. The DNA is arranged into forty-six little packages called chromosomes. Each one contains thousands of genes, which together form the blueprint for how to build and maintain your body. So the chromosomes are like a big set of Do-It-Yourself books, and each gene is like one page in one book, telling you how to build just one tiny part. Only the pages are written in code, and the instructions have to be decoded or translated before they can be used.

So the instructions tell you how to build, what — an arm, or a leg, or a kidney or something?

Not quite. It all starts a little smaller than that. The instructions actually describe how to build proteins, which are biological molecules that do all the really clever stuff in your body.* So, once all the decoding and building are done, you end up with a massive variety of different proteins.

OK . . .

Now everyone has the same basic set of DIY books (or chromosomes), but no two people have exactly the same instructions written on every page. So, compared to some-one else's set, you might be missing an entire page here and there – which means you'll be missing a specific gene, and a specific type of protein. Or the page might have been copied slightly differently, altering the instructions and leaving you with a slightly different gene (and a slightly different pro-tein) to someone else. When this happens, you can end up with blue eyes instead of green eyes, or brown hair instead of blonde hair. So the feature (or *trait*) that the protein controls – like hair or eye colour – can differ. And the trait you end up with depends on which genes are passed down to you from your parents' DIY manuals. Got it?

Think so. But if you were a kid with red hair, and neither of your parents had red hair . . . then . . . like . . . who gave you the red-hair gene?

They both did.

---

* To find out more about how proteins do clever things in the body, see *Do all people see the same colours?* (page 180).

Eh? I don't get that at all.

That's because I left a couple of things out of the story. For starters, not all of the forty-six books in the set are different. In fact, it's more like you have two sets of the same twenty-three-volume series. One set of twenty-three you got from your mother, and the other set of twenty-three you got from your father. So now you have two copies of every book and every page. In other words, you have two copies of each gene – and these copies might be slightly different to each other. Let's call them the 'mum' version and the 'dad' version.

OK. Now what?

Now these two versions of the same gene can interact with each other to produce the hair-colour trait. And, depending on which versions you inherit, they might work together or work against each other. So your 'mum' version and 'dad' version of the gene might *cooperate* to decide your final hair colour, or one might *overrule* the other and decide on its own.

Sounds like mum and dad all right.

They don't *actually* decide, of course – genes are just molecules, and they don't think at all. In reality, the genes and the proteins they build interact in complex ways, producing or blocking chemical reactions within the cell. But the outcome is the same. Genes either cooperate with each other, or one takes over, or *dominates*, the other.

Yup. Still sounds like my parents.

Right. Anyway – here's how it all comes together. The protein that controls whether or not you end up with red hair is called the melanocortin receptor (or MCR) protein, and the instructions for building it are within a gene called MCR1. Got that?

Yup. So far, so good.

Now this protein acts on another proteins – changing their shapes and giving them different functions. In particular, it turns a 'hair reddening' protein (called pheomelanin) into a 'hair darkening' protein (called eumelanin). But remember that you have two versions of each gene—

Mum version, dad version, right?

Right. Now if both versions of your MCR1 gene contain the same, common instructions, then you won't get red hair. This is because you'll make plenty of the MCR protein, which in turn converts the 'reddening' stuff into 'darkening' stuff – darkening your hair overall. We call these common versions 'dominant' and they trump 'recessive' versions of the gene, which have altered instructions – a bit like having spelling mistakes in them. So even if your 'dad' version of the gene is the common (dominant) one, and your 'mum' version has a mistake in it (recessive), you'll still have the correct instructions on board to make the protein that does the darkening job – so no red hair. The 'dad' version takes over, and makes up for the mistakes in the 'mum' version. Got that?

Yeah — think so. Although it's usually my dad that makes the mistakes, and my mum that takes over . . .

Gotcha. But, anyway, you get the idea.

But what if both 'mum' and 'dad' versions have mistakes?

Good question. If that happens, then you have two 'recessive' versions, and no dominant versions of the gene to take up the slack. In that case, the MCR protein doesn't get made properly. Without that, you end up with loads of pheomelanin (hair reddening) protein, and no eumelanin (hair darkening) protein. The un-reddening job isn't done, and you end up with red hair.

So even if your parents have blond and brown hair . . .

. . . then there's still a chance you'll end up with red hair. It just depends which 'mum' and 'dad' versions of the MCR1 gene you inherit. In short, if both your parents give you the recessive versions of the gene, you get red hair. With one brown-haired and one blond-haired parent, there would be roughly a one in four chance of this happening to each child. Other combinations of genes would give you blond or brown hair, but not red. That's the basic pattern, anyway. But it can get a bit more complicated. Want me to explain how?

No, thanks! That'll do me. Lots of genes, lots of different possibilities. Got it. So do genes control other stuff the same way? Like how tall or how clever you are?

Kind of, only those traits involve even more genes, so it gets *a lot* more complicated, and there's a wider range of different results (like different heights or IQs) at the end of it all. Plus, as I said at the beginning, these traits also depend on other things, like your diet and learning experiences, as these affect how well the different proteins work and interact.

So if I want to be taller and cleverer, could I change my genes to do it?

Not right now, as we don't know enough about which genes are involved, or how they interact. Plus it's nearly impossible to change one gene in every one of the billions of cells in your body once you're half-grown already. And although that might become possible some day, there's a much easier way to get the same result.

What's that?

Eat well, study hard and make the most of the genes you've already got.

But I got mine from my brother, and they're all torn and ripped already.

Err . . . that's your *jeans*, not your *genes*.

Oh. I knew that.

Practical science: the difference between genes and jeans

Genes	Jeans
Made of DNA	Made of thick cotton
Roughly 100,000 pairs per person	Most people have only two or three pairs
Blueprint for proteins	Blue denim trousers
Mutant versions have bits missing	Mutant versions have knees, bum missing
Inherited from your parents	Wouldn't be seen dead in your parents' ones

Climate Chaos

Global warming. We hear about it all the time. At home, at school, on the telly, on the Internet – you can't go anywhere without hearing about it. The ice caps are melting . . . the weather's going crazy . . . people and animals are under threat – it's all around us.

It's not surprising, then, that so many of you want to know more about it.

Are we really causing it? What's going to happen? What can we do about it?

With so much information out there, it can all get quite confusing. Even the words people use to talk about it can be different. Like is it 'global warming' or is it 'climate change'?

Well, although many people use the phrase 'global warming', the globe isn't actually heating up evenly all over, like a meatball in the microwave (and some parts of the world are actually cooling). This is why most scientists prefer the phrase 'climate change' – because it better describes what's actually going on. While average surface temperatures are generally going up, the effects differ from place to place. The important thing is how the changes to our climate are affecting weather patterns, sea levels and all forms of life on Earth.

Since it's such a common topic at school, I heard

plenty from you freeloading lazy-boys (and girls) out there:

> You got a question from:
> **Name:** Charlea
> **Question:** Hi Glenn, what are the causes and effects of global warming? Thanks.
>
> You got a question from:
> **Name:** Alina
> **Question:** I have a project about how to save the planet, but I don't have a clue what to write. Can you help me?

So for Charlea, Alina and everyone else who has wondered and worried about clouds, climate change and the atmosphere (and their homework) . . . this one's for you.

When will global warming happen?

Most scientists agree that it's happening already. In fact, it started some time ago – it's just that we've only recently had the methods to spot it.

It's happening already? It doesn't feel like it.

Well, it hasn't gone very far yet. The atmosphere – or at least, the bit of it that we live in near the Earth's surface – has warmed by only around 0.8 °C over the last 100 years. That's too small for most of us to notice. Try putting the heating thermostat in your house up by less than one degree, just for ten minutes or so. Can you feel the difference? Probably not. And that warming happened quickly, taking just minutes. Think about how much harder it would be to spot if the heating took a *century* to raise the room temperature by one degree.

Is that why we can't feel it?

Partly. But the world hasn't warmed evenly either. Some areas of the globe have warmed more than 0.8 °C, and others less. A few areas (like some parts of Antarctica) may even have *cooled* a little over the last century. On top of that, temperatures go up and down with the changing seasons. And shifting ocean current patterns like El Niño and La Niña can cause unusually warm, cool, wet and dry weather in certain regions of the world, and do so quite regularly. All of this masks the slow, steady warming going on in the background. It's only with careful measurements, taken over many years, that scientists have managed to detect the warming at all.*

---

* To find out more, see *How do we know the Earth is warming?* (page 65).

But if we can hardly notice it, then what's the problem? I mean, one degree every hundred years doesn't sound so terrible.

Not to us, perhaps. But even a few degrees' warming can affect the weather, sea levels, wildlife, plant growth, the spread of disease and more. We're seeing signs of this already – right now. In three or four hundred years' time our descendants could live in a very different world to the one we enjoy today. And they probably won't thank us for it. Worse yet – the warming looks like it's speeding up.

Speeding up? Like, how much?

Over the next hundred years, the atmosphere could warm by as much as 5.8 °C. That's over seven times the temperature increase we've seen over the last century.

Yikes! That doesn't sound good at all.

Nope. It isn't.

So will it just keep speeding up until the Earth's frazzled, or will it ever stop?

That's difficult to say. The Earth has warmed like this

before – with global temperatures going up and down again in cycles lasting thousands of years – and this has happened many times over the last four billion years.* Based on what we've figured out about those past times, the warming could speed up, slow down or even reverse itself. It depends what happens to the ice caps, glaciers, oceans and atmosphere as they warm up. But this time it might also depend on what we do to combat it. If we keep burning fossil fuels and increasing our greenhouse gas emissions every year, we're likely to speed the warming up. If we can limit or reduce our emissions, we may have a chance to slow it down. The problem is that the Earth's climate is very complicated, and predicting how it will change – especially far into the future – is incredibly difficult. And without a spare planet (and hundreds of years) to muck about with, scientists can't very well do experiments to see what will happen, as they do with simple physics and chemistry experiments.

So how do the scientists do it, then? Do they just think about it really hard until they get an answer?

They use models.

You mean they ask Kate Moss and Naomi Campbell about it?! I didn't think they were that clever . . .

Err . . . no. I meant they *build* models, and use them to make predictions.

---

* For more about climate change in the Earth's past, see *How do we know the Earth is warming?* (page 65).

Like little planet Earths made out of plastic that they can shine lights on and heat up and stuff?

Close, but a little more advanced. They build computer programs that model the Earth and its climate in 3D, based on real measurements and readings taken by other scientists. They put in numbers for temperatures, gas levels, solar radiation, ice thickness, cloud cover, rainfall and more – fleshing out as much detail as they can to create one huge 'Earth simulator' program. Then they play with it – putting in different figures for, say, the amount of carbon dioxide in the atmosphere, fast-forwarding the simulator, and seeing what that does to global temperatures in 50, 10, or 500 years' time. Or they can raise the temperature and see what effect that has on ice cover, ocean currents, weather patterns, sea levels and so on.

So, basically, one bunch of scientists measures temperatures and stuff all over the world . . .

Right.

. . . and gives their measurements to another bunch of scientists, who play computer games with it.

Right. Only they're very, very complicated and serious games, which are played out on some of the world's most powerful computers. And the results, hopefully, tell us more about how the real world will turn out.

So how do the games end?

Not well, usually. That's how we've come up with the

slightly scary predictions (warming speeding up, sea levels rising) we've heard so far. But not everyone takes these results seriously.

Why not?

Because they're simulations, some people say they don't represent exactly what will happen in the real world. This is true, but they may be the best guess we have as to what *will* happen. For me, that's reason enough to stop and take notice. Because if we play the game badly in real life ...

... then it's 'Game Over'?

Right – and we won't be able to play it again. We've only got one planet, and one chance to play with it. So we'd better play nice ...

How do we know the Earth is warming?

From taking temperature measurements of the land, seas and skies, and from other methods that let us compare today's climate with the climates of the distant past.

I thought scientists still weren't sure whether it was warming or not. That's what I heard on TV, anyway ...

There's a lot on TV and in the news about global warming, and it can all get a bit confusing at times. But it's fair to say that just about *all* climate scientists agree that the Earth's atmosphere is warming. It's just other things they're still not sure about.

Like what?

Like how far it will go – as in *how much* it'll warm up and *how long* the warming will go on for. Also, we're still not certain of what the exact *effects* of warming will be, nor of the best way to *tackle* the whole problem. These are all tricky questions. Scientists have some good theories and suggestions, but it's very difficult to prove any one of them is absolutely correct. In a way, we have to rely on our best guesses. Even the simplest problem – proving the warming exists – hasn't been easy.

Why not? That should be simple, right? Either the Earth's getting warmer or it's not.

Right. But if you want to prove that, you have to measure it. And you can't exactly ask the Earth to say 'ahh' and stick a thermometer in its mouth.

Yeah, but not all thermometers go in the mouth. Some go in the armpit. Or up the bum.

True – but does the Earth have an armpit or a bum?

Err . . . no. S'pose not. So how do you decide where to put the thermometer, then?

Good question. The answer is – you use lots of them, stick them all over the place, then average out the measurements to get an idea of what the real temperature is. On land, we can use temperature gauges in special surface stations that are shielded from direct sunlight, and only measure the air temperature around them. At sea, ships can lower temperature gauges into the water and take readings that way. In the sky, we can use radiosondes (high-altitude balloons carrying thermometers and other sensors) to measure temperatures in different layers of the atmosphere.

We can even take measurements from Space, using satellites. Some special satellites can use microwave detectors to measure the energy given off by gases in the atmosphere, and climatologists (scientists who study the climate and how it changes) can use these readings to work out atmospheric temperatures. Some can even be used to measure land and sea surface temperatures using similar methods. But none of these readings alone can give the temperature of the entire atmosphere. There are hot spots and cold spots in different places on Earth, and shifting weather patterns move warm and cool air around in the atmosphere. So, to get an accurate figure, climatologists combine all these results and average them out in different ways.

OK — so that shows the world is *warm*, maybe. But how do we know it's still warming?

Well, firstly, we've been taking many of these measurements for over fifty years, and even in that short time we've seen an increase in average temperature in parts of the atmosphere. Secondly, there's another set of methods that lets us deduce what temperatures were like in the past – even millions of years ago.

How could we ever know that?

Using clues. Different types of clues, from different sources. Then seeing whether the clues agree with each other.

Like a police detective?

Right – just like that. You gather clues, put them together and hopefully solve the mystery. Only here the mystery isn't a crime – it's the true story of the Earth's atmosphere and climate.

So what are the clues?

One kind comes from living things. You might have heard that counting rings in a felled tree can tell you how old it was. Well, if you know how to read them, tree rings can also tell you how fast the tree grew each year, which can tell you something about how warm the climate was, and maybe even how much carbon dioxide was in the atmosphere at the time (since both these things affect how fast trees and plants will grow). Some corals and shellfish have growth patterns like this too – so we can also use old (even fossilized) animals to deduce things about ancient climates.

Other clues come from rocks, some of which geologists can analyse to tell how much ice was present millions of years ago – which itself can tell us how warm (or cold) it must have been at certain times in the Earth's history. And the ancient ice that's still around – especially in the Antarctic ice sheet – can give us still more clues.

How's that, then?

Thick sheet ice is formed over thousands of years, as thin layers of snow fall each year and become compressed into rock-hard ice. Bubbles of air from the atmosphere are trapped in each layer. Today, climate scientists can drill into these layers, remove long cylinders (or ice cores) and analyse the bubbles to see which gases were present at different times. Taken together, these things can also tell us how warm it was.

So there are plenty of clues. You just have to know how to read them. And the story they tell is quite clear – the Earth's atmosphere has warmed and cooled before, but right now it's warming *a lot*, and it's warming *very quickly*.

So why aren't we doing more to stop it?

Because although we have a good idea of what's been *causing* the warming, we still can't be completely certain we're right. Which leaves plenty of room for people to argue about what (if anything) we should do about it.

But we know the world's warming ...

Yup.

... and we're pretty sure that's *bad* ...

Yup.

Then we should definitely do *something*.

Right. And we are. We're finding out more, and we're making plans to stop (or cut down on) doing some of the things we think might be causing the warming.

But will that be enough?

Good question. Let's hope so. Or let's do more about it ...

Sci-facts: what are we doing?

Since 1988, the governments of the world have been working together to find out more about climate change, and to figure out how to tackle it. Here's a brief list of what they've done so far:

1988   The United Nations (UN) forms the International Panel on Climate Change (IPCC) – an international group dedicated to gathering reliable information about climate change from scientists worldwide and reporting it to the world's governments.

1992   166 countries work together to produce and sign the UN Framework Convention on Climate Change (UNFCCC), which asks each country to measure their own greenhouse gas emissions and, if they're found to be too high, to do something about them.

1997   UN countries meet in Kyoto, Japan, and agree targets for limiting greenhouse gas emissions – creating the famous Kyoto Protocol.

1998–2004   The Kyoto Protocol is signed by all but a few countries, and many start effectively reducing their emissions.

2005   The Kyoto Protocol becomes international law, to be enforced until 2012.

2007, 2008, 2009 . . .   UN countries continue to meet at conferences and summit meetings to agree what to do next, once the Kyoto Protocol has run out . . .

Is the world warming on its own, or are we doing it?

The Earth's climate has both warmed and cooled in the past, and most of these changes had 'natural' causes like volcanoes, asteroids and the Sun. But these can't explain the warming we've seen lately, which suggests we're probably to blame for it.

Why us, though? I mean, couldn't it just be the Sun's fault?

As in, the Sun warms the Earth, the Earth's getting warmer, so maybe the Sun's just getting hotter?

Right.

That does seem obvious, and the Sun has definitely been involved in some warming and cooling of the Earth's climate in the past. Its temperature (or rather, the amount of energy it puts out) has gone up and down from time to time, and this has probably caused fast warming and cooling of the climate before.

There — you see?

Plus, the Earth's orbit round the Sun has shifted over time, and so has the tilt of its axis (the line running from the North to the South Pole, which the Earth spins round). This moves parts of the Earth (the Arctic, for example) towards or away from the Sun for long stretches of time, shifting back and forth in cycles that last thousands of years. In turn, this causes an alternating pattern of heating and cooling, which melts and refreezes polar ice, giving regular ice ages (during the freezes) with long periods of slow global warming in between.

So that's it, then. Sorted. It's just the Sun and the Earth doing their thing.

Well, unfortunately it doesn't look like it this time. These natural shifts happen very slowly – over thousands of years – and they can't explain the rapid warming we've seen since the 1970s. Something else must be doing it.

What about volcanoes? What's the deal with them?

Volcanoes spew out dust, carbon dioxide and other gases that affect global warming too, and once in a while a very large eruption will spit so much ash into the high atmosphere that it can envelop the globe and block out the sun for a year or more. After the Indonesian volcano Krakatoa erupted in 1883, temperatures dropped by more than 1° C for over a year, and weather patterns were affected for another four years after that.

And asteroids?

Likewise, a large asteroid striking the Earth can create an immense explosion that throws steam, dust and ash into the atmosphere, having similar effects (or worse) to that of a volcanic eruption. An asteroid like this hit Chicxulub in Mexico around 65 million years ago, exploding with more force than *seven billion* atomic bombs. This may have affected the climate for years afterwards, killing off animal and plant species across the globe, including – many scientists believe – most of the dinosaurs.

Couldn't they have changed the climate?

Maybe, but big eruptions and asteroid strikes generally cause cooling, rather than the warming we've seen lately. And volcanoes haven't puffed out nearly enough greenhouse gases to cause *all* (or even most) of the recent warming either. So, while volcanoes, asteroids and the Sun have all played their parts in climate change, none of these 'natural causes' can explain the changes in global temperature we've spotted over the last thirty or forty years.

So if we're pretty sure the warming's not natural, why do some people keep saying it is?

For two reasons.

First, it's hard to *prove* what the real cause is. We can prove that we've altered the Earth's atmosphere by burning coal, gas and oil. We can prove that the atmosphere has been warming. But, however obvious it might seem, we can't prove with complete accuracy that the burning *caused* the warming.

And the other reason?

The second reason is – some people just don't want to know. Admitting that the problem is our fault means we have to change the way we run our lives, our businesses – even our countries – to try and fix it. Some people *really* don't want to do that, so they refuse to believe we're the problem, or avoid talking about it. That way, they don't have to do anything. Others realize there's a problem, but think it'll be too difficult or costly to make changes. This is particularly a problem in developing countries, where people find it harder to make costly changes than people in developed countries.

But it's still happening! And they're making it worse!

Yup. It's a tough one.

What do we do about it?

Well, we just keep on talking about it until everyone understands. Or at least until enough people get the message to make a difference.

Can I talk about it?

Absolutely. Go for it.

Talk about it, read about it, learn about it – save the world!

Can we stop the greenhouse effect and global warming?

We can't stop the greenhouse effect, and we wouldn't want to. It keeps us all alive and without it the Earth would be a very different place. Global warming caused by humans, however, is another story ...

But aren't the greenhouse effect and global warming the same thing?

Not quite. The greenhouse effect is a process that makes (and keeps) the Earth a lot warmer than it would otherwise be, by trapping infrared radiation – otherwise known as heat – in the atmosphere. Normally this keeps the Earth at a fairly stable, toasty temperature. Global warming is what happens when the greenhouse effect gets kicked up a notch. This causes temperatures to drift steadily upwards over time, creating all kinds of problems for things attempting to live on the planet. Like us.

So the greenhouse effect *causes* global warming, right? No greenhouse effect, no warming.

That's true, but ...

There you go, you see? All you have to do is stop the greenhouse effect, and the problem's sorted.

All right, then – let's say you're right. How would you go about doing that?

Ha! Easy! I've got a master plan. Can't fail.

Off you go, then. Fire away.

You just block out the Sun and cool everything off.

With what?

With, like, a massive sunshade in Space, between us and the Sun. You could carry it there in a rocket.

OK, let's say you can build it big enough to blot out the Sun, leaving the Earth in complete shadow . . .

Right!

. . . then you've just created a permanent worldwide solar eclipse. Soon, the world will freeze, killing everything on it. Not a good result, all told.

Oh. Oops. OK, then — Plan B.

Plan B?

Yeah — Plan B. You build an enormous vacuum cleaner and suck all the gases out of the atmosphere, so they can't trap heat.

All the gases? You don't want to leave a little air behind, maybe?

Right, right . . . not *all* the gases. Just the ones that cause the greenhouse effect. That's what I meant.

OK, but even if your greenhouse-gas-filtering megahoover does the job, you've still got a problem.

What's that?

The major greenhouse gases in the atmosphere – water vapour and carbon dioxide – also happen to be essential for life on Earth. Remove those, and all the plants and algae die since they (and also many kinds of bacteria) need water and carbon dioxide to grow and survive. Once they died, all the other organisms that feed on them would follow soon after.

. . . That's if they could survive long enough to starve in the freezing temperatures. By removing carbon dioxide and other greenhouse gases, you would successfully stop the greenhouse effect from happening. But unfortunately that would leave the Earth at an average temperature of – 18 °C. Something like northern Siberia is now.

So, basically, we can't stop the greenhouse effect. And, even if we could, it would be a really bad idea.

In short, yes. The greenhouse effect is essential for all life on the planet as it keeps temperatures within the narrow range we and other organisms need to survive. We don't want to stop it happening. That said, we don't want it to run away with itself either – that would be almost as bad as having it stop.

And that's global warming?

Right. That's what all the fuss is about. For over 150 years, we've been adding enormous amounts of carbon dioxide and other greenhouse gases to the atmosphere – mostly by burning oil, gas and coal to produce energy. This seems to have driven global temperatures up by amplifying the greenhouse effect. So it's more like global *heating* than global warming. It's not just happening – we're doing it.

So can't we just stop heating it by not adding any more gases to the atmosphere?

Ah – there's the problem, you see. That would mean not burning any more coal, gas or oil. We've come to depend on these fuels for electricity, heating and transport. So we can't just stop using them tomorrow. Not without an alternative way of powering our homes, factories, offices and vehicles. Alternative energy sources* – like solar, wind, hydroelectric and biomass power – do exist, but they're not developed enough to take over from fossil fuels completely. Nuclear power is another option, but that comes with some of its own problems (like how to get rid of the dangerous radioactive waste it creates). So the best we can do is cut down on burning fossil fuels as much as we can while we try to develop alternative energy sources – ones that can power our future without increasing the greenhouse effect. Until that's done, the problem will be getting worse all the time.

Sounds like we'd better work fast.

You said it!

---

* For more about alternative energy sources, see *Could we use animal poo in power stations to make electricity?* (page 99).

Do cow farts cause climate change?

Stinky as they are, cow farts do little to affect climate change. But cow *burps* are another matter. Along with those of other grazing animals, they're definitely adding to the climate change problem.

So farts don't cause climate change, but burps do?

Actually, neither farts nor burps actually *causes* it. Climate change is the result of many different things affecting the Earth, and cow gases are just one part of the big picture. It's all to do with the amounts of greenhouse gases that have built up in the atmosphere, and how that has been trapping more and more heat.

So why burps but not farts?

Because cow farts, while stinky, do not contain much in the way of greenhouse gases (well – no more than the farts of most other animals, including us). But because of the

way they digest things, cows and other grazing animals do produce greenhouse gases from the *other* end – when they belch or burp.

Do cows burp carbon dioxide, then?

Well, yes. But that's not the problem. All animals produce carbon dioxide when they breathe (and burp), and also when they die and decompose.

Hang on — I thought carbon dioxide was a big problem for global warming and stuff?

You're right – it is. But the carbon dioxide produced naturally by living organisms is more than balanced out by *other* living organisms – the plants, algae and bacteria that *absorb* carbon dioxide during photosynthesis. It's the carbon dioxide we've produced artificially – through burning coal, gas and oil – that has thrown the whole cycle out of whack. This carbon dioxide from fossil fuels dwarfs the amount that cows and other living things produce each day. So cow-burp carbon isn't the problem.

So what's the big problem with cows?

The problem is that there are other gases causing problems in the atmosphere – some many times more powerful and damaging than carbon dioxide. And one of these is found in cow burps too. Cows, sheep and other grazing animals (or ruminants) burp methane – a very powerful greenhouse gas. Ruminants, you see, eat grass. Grass is hard to digest, so they have to chew it, swallow it, digest it in their stomachs for a bit, then bring it back up, chew it some more . . .

Yuck!

. . . Wait for it – then repeat this process again and again until the bacteria living in their stomachs have broken down the squidgy lump of pulped grass inside their bodies. In the process, they release methane. When this gets into the atmosphere, it absorbs up to twenty-five times more heat than carbon dioxide does. So even though there's a lot less of it (only two parts per million – 190 times less than the amount of carbon dioxide in the atmosphere), the impact methane has on global warming is about one third that of all the carbon dioxide.

So methane is the worst ever greenhouse gas?

It's pretty bad, but there are some even more powerful gases up ther, too. Chlorofluorocarbons, or CFCs, are man-made gases used since the 1920s in aerosol spray-cans, fridges and air-conditioners. As greenhouse gases, they are about *2,000 times* more powerful than carbon dioxide. So, even though there isn't a great deal of CFC gas in the atmosphere, the stuff that we've already put there is doing a lot of damage. Thankfully, we've been creating and releasing less of these each year since 1987, when the countries of the world figured out CFCs were also destroying the ozone layer, and decided together to cut back on them. There are a few other powerful gases too, like nitrous oxide and near-surface ozone, which are mostly produced by factories, vehicles and farming. And even water vapour is a greenhouse gas. It's a pretty weak one compared to the others, but because there's so much of it in the atmosphere (almost thirty times more than there is carbon dioxide), it has an enormous effect. And it might cause even more problems later on as more and more water will be evaporated off the oceans as the atmosphere heats up.

So how much methane do cows actually burp out?

A single cow burps 80 to 110kg of methane every year.

That doesn't sound so much.

Maybe not. Until you multiply it by the number of cows around. There are over *100 million* cattle in the USA alone, and about *1.2 billion* grass-chewing, methane-burping cows, sheep, goats and other ruminants across the globe. Together, they belch out over 80 million tonnes of methane each year.

OK, that's a lot of burp . . .

Yup. It's a good thing methane is odourless, or the world might be quite a bit stinkier.

Can we do anything about it?

Well, you can't very well ask over a billion animals to stop burping. And unless you kept them all indoors, or fitted them all with burp-catching gas masks – neither of which is likely to happen – you couldn't hope to capture the methane before it made it into the atmosphere. And, even if we did catch all the cow burps (or simply stopped breeding cows), this wouldn't really solve the methane problem.

Why not?

Because, for starters, wild ruminants burp just as much as the ones we breed ourselves, and there would be plenty more of them around to keep on burping. And, even if you got rid of them (not a very nice thing to do, even in the interests of saving the planet), the vast majority of methane released into the atmosphere each year comes from other sources, including bacteria, termites, plants, human waste dumps and sewerage works. Plants alone produce between 10% and 30% (60 million to 180 million tonnes) of the methane released per year.

What?! But I thought plants and trees were good things. Don't they help stop the greenhouse effect?

Yup. Exactly right.

So what can we do?

Well, looking at the options, we can't get rid of the cows, sheep, goats and other ruminants. We probably couldn't get rid of the termites and bacteria even if we wanted to (there are just too many of them). And we can't get rid of the plants. So that leaves the human methane sources – waste dumps and sewerage works. We can reduce the methane released from waste dumps by creating less waste and by recycling as much as we can of what's left. And scientists are working on new ways of treating waste and sewage that reduces the amount of methane they produce – maybe even use it as a fuel (or biogas) to generate power!*

---

* For more about methane and using bioenergy, see *Could we use animal poo in power stations to make electricity?* (page 99).

So we power the world with rubbish and poo, and cows are free to burp like you and me?

Err . . . right. Something like that.

Weird. But cool.

Yup. That's science for ya – weird, but cool.

What are clouds for?

Clouds might seem to be just annoying bringers of bad weather, but they're also very helpful. We can use them to navigate, and to forecast weather. They form a handy natural sunscreen. And, most importantly, they bring us fresh water – without which we could not survive.

Pah. No they don't. Clouds are rubbish. All they do is mess up sunny days and pelt you with rain.

Actually, only some of them do. Many types of cloud form and evaporate without ever raining on us at all. Others form huge, towering masses that pelt us with rain, hail and worse. It all depends how and where they form, and how they grow and develop.

Aren't clouds all the same?

In one way – yes, they are. They're all made of water vapour, which is a gas made of water molecules (as opposed to a solid or liquid – which we would call 'ice' and 'water'). Water vapour is almost always present in the air around us (the amount ranges from 0% to 7%, depending on how humid it is), but usually the molecules are spread out so it's invisible. As the land and seas warm up, they also warm the air above them, causing pockets of warm air to rise and expand and take some water vapour up with them. These warm air pockets eventually drift up into cooler regions of the atmosphere further away from the ground.* When this happens, the water vapour cools

---

* For more about the layers of the Earth's atmosphere, see *Why can't aeroplanes fly into Space?* (page 133).

and the water molecules stick together, forming millions of tiny water droplets. This is what we call a cloud.

So why don't we see it rising up? Why do we only see the cloud once it's up there?

Because water vapour lets light rays go straight through it, so it's invisible. But water molecules in clouds are more densely packed. That means they scatter light rays passing through them, like millions of tiny mirrors. So by the time the light reaches us on the ground, it seems to come from everywhere in the cloud at once, and the cloud appears white.

OK, but they're not always white. Sometimes they're grey, or even black. Especially the nasty ones.

That's true. And that's partly due to whether the sun is behind them or not. But it's also due to how big each cloud gets, and how much water it can hold. Most clouds start out more or less the same, but how a cloud grows will decide what *species* (or type) of cloud it will turn into, and how it behaves. Your basic 'ball of cotton wool' cloud is called a cumulus. These clouds form over heated columns of air, as described above, and generally just sit there looking pretty. But if they continue to grow higher into the atmosphere, they can turn into a cumulonimbus – the huge, dark, menacing-looking clouds that cause storms of all kinds.

What, like thunderstorms?

Yup. Plus hailstorms, ice storms, and – if they gang up together in massive supercell formations – hurricanes, typhoons or cyclones. If the conditions are right, they can even reach down with spinning cloud funnels (otherwise known as tornadoes) to wipe trees, buildings or even entire towns off the landscape. In all, they're not too friendly, as clouds go . . .

Told you so.

. . . but the cumulonimbus is only one type of cloud, and most of the rest – including cirrus, stratus and other types of cloud – are harmless. In fact, some are very useful, or even helpful to us.

How's that?

For starters, you can use clouds to navigate. Out at sea, cumulus clouds often form right above small islands, because the land is usually warmer than the sea around it. So sailors on the open ocean can spot these clouds before seeing the land itself, and use them to find land. To an airline pilot, a cloud can be a tell-tale sign of a rising air pocket – the kind that causes turbulence. So, by recognizing their shapes, pilots can navigate through a sea of clouds and avoid the 'roughest' patches to give the passengers a smooth ride. Clouds also form a convenient sunscreen, protecting us from the full glare and heat of the sun. On average, clouds scatter about 20% of the Sun's rays and absorb another 19%. Without them, the land, seas and atmosphere would be much warmer during the day (although they also trap heat in the lower atmosphere at night, so scientists aren't yet sure how they affect global warming).*

---

* For more about the greenhouse effect, see *Can we really stop the greenhouse effect and global warming?* (page 74).

All right — clouds aren't *all* bad. But I could still do without them.

Actually, you probably couldn't. None of us could. Without clouds and rain there would be no fresh water.

Yes, there would. You could get it from a well, or a lake or something.

OK . . . but where do you think the fresh water in those comes from?

Err — from rain, I guess. Or a river. Up a mountain or a hill somewhere.

Right. And to get *there*, it had to be carried by clouds. Without clouds, there would be no rivers, no lakes, no streams and no reservoirs. All the fresh water would be permanently locked up underground or in the atmosphere. And, since seawater is too salty to drink, that'd do you no good, either. You can get fresh water from the sea (by boiling, condensing and filtering it), but it's hard work, and it wouldn't be easy to make enough for everybody this way. Thankfully, clouds do all this for us – carrying trillions of tonnes of water over land and dumping it on higher ground to form streams and rivers. All we have to do is build our towns and cities near one, and we're sorted. That's why, if you think about it, pretty much every city in the world is built on or near at least one large river (have a look at the box on page 88, if you don't believe me). Without a river, all those city folk couldn't stay well watered for long.

Oh yeah. Hadn't thought of that.

There you go, you see? Clouds are like a big, fluffy, conveyor belt in the sky – bringing you water, for free, all year round. So next time you look up and see a cloudy sky, be happy about it. Unless it's a massive cumulonimbus right overhead, of course.

What should I do then?

Be happy about it from a distance. Or indoors.

Sci-facts: world rivers

City	River
Cairo	Nile
London	Thames
Paris	Seine
Rome	Tiber
Shanghai	Huangpu
Tokyo	Sumida
Moscow	Moskva
Melbourne	Yarra
Bangkok	Chao Phraya
New York	Hudson

Is global warming messing with the weather?

It's difficult to tell, and not easy to prove, but many scientists think global warming could *really* mess with the weather in the future, and may already be doing it.

So what kind of weather does it make?

Global warming doesn't really make or create any kind of weather, but it will cause some existing types of weather to become more severe and, like I said, we may be seeing signs of that already.*

Is that why we're getting more heatwaves and hurricanes and earthquakes and stuff?

Why do you say that?

It seems that way. There's always one of those on the telly these days.

Well, it's true that certain types of extreme weather seem to be on the increase, but it's a little more complicated than that. Global warming doesn't amplify *all* types of weather and natural disasters. Earthquakes, for example, have little or nothing to do with climate change. Nor do tidal waves (like the recent Asian tsunami). We're just hearing more about them lately because they're recorded and reported more often than they used to be. That said, heatwaves do seem to be getting worse.

---

* For more about how climate change may change the world, see *If our climate changes, where will be the best and worst places to live?* (page 106).

Like, they're hotter than before?

Not so much hotter – the highest temperatures reached are about the same as before. But they do seem to be lasting longer, which is causing real problems in some areas, such the Mediterranean region. Thousands of people in France, Spain, Italy and Greece have been rushed to hospital over the last few summers, suffering from heatstroke. The very young and older people have suffered worst, as scorching temperatures have gone on for days and stayed unusually high at night, giving people no chance to cool down and recover.

What about hurricanes? There've been loads of them lately . . .

That's true, there have been a lot over the last few years (including a record fifteen hurricanes in 2005). And although we're still not sure whether global warming is to blame, the signs are not good. In the last hundred years, the average number of tropical storms per year has more than doubled – from about six a year in 1900 to about fifteen per year over the last decade. (In 2005, there were twenty-eight – of which fifteen went on to become hurricanes.)

Why does global warming affect hurricanes, anyway? I mean, I understand heatwaves, as that's just the air heating up. But why would more heat cause bigger storms?

Because all storms – including massive ones like hurricanes – are fed by warm water evaporating off the ocean. And global warming doesn't just heat up the land, it also warms the seas, causing shifts in the ocean currents that drive weather patterns across the globe. Tropical cyclones (hurricanes, cyclones and typhoons) form in the warm waters around the equator, where the ocean gets the most constant sunlight. After they form, they move north or south from the equator, passing over cooler waters before striking land – often in the same places every year, such as the Caribbean Islands, the south coast of the USA, Japan and the Philippines. Global warming may be keeping the waters around these hurricane and typhoon 'hotspots' warmer than usual, feeding the storms and making them bigger and more powerful. Which isn't good news for people who have to cope with them.

What about tornadoes? Does it cause them too?

Nope – they're different. Tornadoes usually form in special types of thunderstorms called supercells, and there's no sign of those getting more frequent as the atmosphere warms. Again, people have just been taking more notice of them lately (especially since the Hollywood disaster movie *Twister* came out in 2000!) so they're making their way into the news more often than before.

What about the other kinds of weather-weirdness?

Well, it's hard to know for sure, but it seems fairly likely that the steady heating of the oceans may eventually lead to some changes in global *ocean–atmosphere cycles* – like the famous El Niño cycle, more properly called the *El Niño Southern Oscillation* or *ENSO*. Every two to seven years, El Niño affects weather patterns throughout the southern hemisphere, causing droughts in Indonesia, Australia, South Africa and South America. It may also cause more hurricanes in the Atlantic (but fewer typhoons in the Pacific). If the oceans warm too much, some scientists think that El Niño could set in permanently, leaving constant droughts in those regions it affects, and causing more and more Atlantic hurricanes every year.

That doesn't sound good.

Nope.

So can we stop climate change from messing with the weather?

Not really – since climate and weather are so closely linked, if one changes, the other is bound to also. The only way to prevent weather change is to try and prevent more climate change from happening.

And let me guess — that won't be too easy?

Nope – but we can give it a shot!

Will global warming hurt animals?

Unfortunately, it looks like it will. Climate changes affect some animals more than others, so while many will survive, animal life on our planet will be a lot less varied if global warming continues.

How do we know it'll affect animals?

Partly from what scientists have seen already. Every few years, the World Conservation Union gathers information from biologists studying animals all around the world. From this data, they estimate how many of the world's known animal (and also plant and fungus) species are low enough in number to be threatened or endangered. Their most recent reports have found that over 16,000 species are now threatened with extinction. This includes around one in eight bird species, one in five mammals and one in three amphibians (frogs, toads, newts and salamanders).

But don't animals go extinct because of hunting and killing?

That's true – species can become extinct that way, and some have in the past. But the vast majority of species become extinct through changes to their environment that happen too quickly for them to deal with. And that's what's happening now.

Couldn't they just adapt to living in a hotter world? Like, evolve or something?

Some will, but others won't be able to in time. The problem is that, for most species, it isn't just the climbing temperature that's killing them. It's the destruction of their habitat – which has been going on for a long time in many parts of the world. On top of that, climate change is like the last straw – the thing that finishes off a species that's already in trouble.

Is this happening to animals already, then?

Yes – it seems to be. And in habitats all over the world.

The pika, for example, is a cute, hamster-like animal that lives on rocky mountain tops across Asia and North America. Over the last eighty years, its numbers have dropped rapidly as the pika has been unable to cope with the rising air temperatures at high altitudes. It has disappeared altogether in many places, and is thought to be headed for extinction.

The golden toad, which lives only in the forests of Costa Rica, is another victim of climate change. This species may already be extinct – killed off by a fungus that spread more quickly through its habitat as the forest nights became warmer.

In the Arctic, polar bear numbers have been dropping as global warming gradually melts the ice floes they live on – preventing them from hunting the seals they need to survive.

That's so sad.

Yes. It is.

So what do we do about it?

We save as many of them as we can.

How do we do that?

By protecting their habitats and setting up refuge areas (where people are not allowed to hunt, cut down trees or build houses or farms).

But how will we know where to put these?

To decide that, we have to look at where *most* of the species actually are.

What do you mean?

Well, animal species are not spread evenly around the globe. Over half the animal species we know of live on just 2% of the Earth's surface – in species 'hotspots' like the forests of Brazil, Madagascar, Hawaii and the Philippines. Unfortunately, many of these areas are also the most threatened with destruction, as people cut down trees for timber or burn them to clear the ground for farmland. 70–90% of all endangered animals live within hotspots like this. So by protecting these areas we can protect the largest number of species from extinction, and preserve the variety of living things (or *biodiversity*) on Earth for the future.

But what about the rest of the animals — like the polar bears and pikas?

The best thing we can do for them is take steps to combat climate change itself, by conserving energy, recycling materials, cutting down our use of fossil fuels and developing alternative energy sources. After all, we kind of owe it to them – since we're the only animal on the planet that caused the climate change problem in the first place.*

And it's not like the other animals could fix it for themselves . . .

Right. It's all up to us.

---

* For more about combating climate change, see *Can we really stop the greenhouse effect and global warming?* (page 74).

Sci-facts: endangered animals

Animals are threatened by global warming in different ways. Many mammals and birds are suffering as the plants that make up their food sources and habitats fail to thrive. Many reptiles and amphibians are also suffering as the climate becomes too hot or too cold for them to handle (remember – climate change could make some parts of the world colder, rather than hotter). Meanwhile, changing sea temperatures and ocean currents are affecting fish and other marine creatures.

Of all the species studied in these groups, the numbers below show how many species are currently endangered, due to climate change and other reasons:

Reptiles	1 in 20 species
Fish	1 in 20 species
Birds	1 in 8 species
Mammals	1 in 5 species
Amphibians	1 in 3 species

Could we use animal poo in power stations to make electricity?

Yes! Poo-power is already in use in some places, and one day we might be able to use it to power our cars and buses too. What's more, poo-power and other forms of bioenergy could even help save the planet!

Poo-powered buses?! How would that work? Would you have to get everyone to poo in the fuel tank as they get on?

Err, no – that's not quite . . .

. . . or maybe there's just a hole in the seat, and . . .

Ugh! Stop it! That's not how it'd work at all!

It isn't?

No! The cars and buses wouldn't *run* on poo. They'd be electric,* or hydrogen-powered. But you could make that electricity and hydrogen *using* poo-power and other sources of bioenergy.

Oh. So what's bioenergy, then?

It's a form of renewable energy that you get from burning organic matter or the gases it produces.

---

* For more about electric cars, see *If normal car engines cause pollution, why don't we all use electric ones?* (page 146).

Like those vegetables you buy at the supermarket?

No – not that kind of organic. 'Organic' just means 'living' – so it's anything that's produced from living things. This includes solid fuels – such as trees, plants, wood, paper and 'animal waste' (i.e. poo). These are called biomass fuels. But it also includes gaseous fuels, such as methane, which comes off plants and animal bodies and heaps of manure as they burn or rot. These are called biogases. Both biomass and biogases can be used to produce energy in two ways. The simplest way is to burn them to create heat for warmth. (So, in a way, our prehistoric ancestors were using one biomass fuel this way tens of thousands of years ago, by burning twigs and branches.) Alternatively, you can burn them to heat water, generate steam and spin electricity-producing turbines in power stations.

Then what?

Then you can use that energy to heat and power homes, businesses, factories and electric vehicles. You could even use it to create hydrogen fuels from water, and that could one day be used to run hydrogen-powered cars, trains and maybe even aeroplanes. Many scientists think this might be a powerful way of reducing our use of fossil fuels, decreasing our carbon emissions and protecting the environment from the perils of global warming. (You might also remember that methane is a powerful greenhouse gas* once released into the high atmosphere. So burning it at ground level has the added bonus of preventing this greenhouse bad-boy from getting up there.)

---

* For more about how global warming works, see *Is the world warming on its own, or are we doing it?* (page 70).

Hang on — don't coal and oil come from dead animals and plants too?

They do.

So what's the difference between burning those and burning twigs and animal poo?

Good point. In short, twigs and animal poo contain much less carbon than fossil fuels, so release a lot less carbon dioxide when you burn them. Fossil fuels are formed from huge numbers of dead plants and animals – their bodies packed together and fossilized over millions of years.

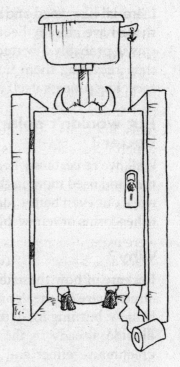

Think of it this way – when you burn a tree, you burn one plant containing a few decades' worth (maybe a few hundred years' worth at most) of carbon. When you burn a lump of coal, you're burning what was once a huge number of plants, and releasing millions of years' worth of stored carbon . . . all at once. And that's not even considering all the energy used (and carbon dioxide released) when the coal was mined in the first place.

But I thought chopping down trees and burning them was bad for the environment.

Not if you plant new ones just for that purpose, and replace the ones you cut down. Plus, you can burn *recycled* tree material like wood and paper – since the trees that made those have already been chopped down anyway. In fact, this is probably a better way of reusing wood and paper than recycling them into more wood and paper, as the recycling process itself uses energy (and releases carbon).

But wouldn't solar power or wind power be better?

Well, we're certainly hoping that they'll be developed further and used more in the future too. But bioenergy could work out even better for the environment than these and other forms of renewable energy.

Why?

Because of how these different forms of power affect the atmosphere as they're produced. As you probably know by now, burning fossil fuels adds to the amount of carbon dioxide already in the atmosphere, which fires up the greenhouse effect and causes global warming. Because burning fossil fuels adds carbon to the atmosphere, we call these *carbon-positive* energy sources. Wind, solar and many other forms of renewable energy are a better alternative, since they can be used to generate energy without releasing carbon dioxide. As they neither add nor remove carbon from the atmosphere, we call these *carbon-neutral* energy sources.

OK . . .

But bioenergy fuels can go one better. The trees and plants that are planted to create biomass fuels actually *remove* carbon from the atmosphere. Provided you capture the carbon dioxide released as you burn them, that means some (not all, but some) bioenergy fuels have the promise of being *carbon-negative* fuels. Using them could not only halt the damage we've already caused to the atmosphere, but could also help *undo* it by removing huge amounts of carbon that we've already released. As for poo, letting it rot releases methane – which is a powerful greenhouse gas in itself. So burning the poo (or the methane biogas that comes off it) before it can rot also decreases the amount of greenhouse gases in the atmosphere.

Wouldn't burning poo be a bit — you know — stinky?

Well, along with the carbon dioxide released as you burn the poo, you could capture the smelly sulphurous gases that cause the stink at the power station. That way, you could avoid replacing air pollution with poo-llution. Of course, you've still got the problem of where you're going to put all those captured gases. One idea is to pipe the carbon dioxide into the same undersea pits that oil rigs extract oil from, and seal them up. Then we'd just have to hope no one accidentally drilled into them in the future. Same goes for the smelly sulphur gases – you could pipe them somewhere safe too. Unless you were feeling particularly evil, of course (see table on page 105).

So if poo-power and bioenergy are so great, why aren't we using them already?

As a matter of fact, we are! In the UK, over half of our renewable energy comes from biomass energy and biofuels (the rest coming from wind, wave, hydroelectric and solar power). A power plant in Suffolk, England, uses the poo from local chicken farms to supply local towns with energy. The poo from 100,000 chickens can be turned into enough energy to heat 10,000 homes! The largest biomass power plant in the world, which will run on woodchips, is being built in Wales. Similar power stations using chicken poo, pig poo or wood chippings are being built in America and Australia.

Yeah, but if it's that great, we should be using it everywhere. Right now.

Maybe. But, right now, we still have oil, gas and coal left. So most countries are still depending on those, and bioenergy development is going fairly slowly. But once the fossil fuels run out that might increase the pressure on many countries to start using alternatives. And as bioenergy helps reduce greenhouse gas emissions, more countries may adopt it to try and stay under the low-carbon limits set during the Kyoto Protocol and other international agreements. We may never be able to power the entire world with plants and poo alone. But combined with other forms of renewable energy, poo and other biomass fuels could lead the way to a cleaner energy future.

Weird.

What's that?

Never thought you could use poo to clean something up!

Practical science: top 10 places to which you could pipe the stinky gases captured from burning poo (just for a laugh)

1 Your brother's bedroom
2 Your sister's bedroom
3 Your dad's shed
4 Your neighbour's greenhouse
5 The *Big Brother* house
6 The school canteen
7 The teachers' staff room
8 The head teacher's office
9 The gym changing room
10 The boys'/girls' toilets

If our climate changes, where will be the worst and best places to live?

We can't know for sure, but the worst places may be the lowest, wettest and driest areas of the planet. The best places may be the high spots, and places where the weather changes very little.

The wettest *and* the driest places? That can't be right.

Why not?

It has to be one or the other. You can't have both.

OK – let's think about it for a minute. If the atmosphere keeps on warming, what kinds of changes might happen to the Earth?

The land gets hotter and dries out. Deserts everywhere.

Right. In some places, this will happen – and it may already be happening. Parts of Africa, Australia, Indonesia and South America have seen some of their worst ever droughts in recent years, and many scientists think global warming is to blame. Anything else?

All the ice melts and the sea levels rise. Places near the sea get flooded.

Right. Although it's unlikely that *all* the ice will melt, melting big enough chunks of Greenland and the Antarctic ice sheet will be enough to raise sea levels worldwide. If this happens, many low-lying islands and coastal areas will be under threat from flooding. Again, this may already be happening. The sea level has risen by about 20cm over the last hundred years, causing higher and more frequent floods in islands throughout the Pacific and Indian Oceans. People living on the Pacific island of Tuvalu, in fact, may soon have to evacuate to Fiji or New Zealand to escape the rising seas.

OK — so that's why the driest places and the lowest places won't be great to live in. But why the wettest? I don't get that at all.

Well, we've talked about the land and the ice caps, but what lies between them?

Err . . . seawater. Lots of it.

Right. And what happens when you heat up water?

You get steam?

Exactly. It evaporates and turns into water vapour.

Hang on a minute — are you telling me it's going to get so hot that the oceans are going to boil?

No, not at all. But they don't have to. Seawater turns into water vapour all the time as water molecules at the surface warm up, break free of the water and move into the air, eventually forming clouds. Then these clouds of water vapour turn back into liquid water and fall to Earth as they cool down – creating rain. A warmer atmosphere can hold more water vapour, and creates more clouds. So, as the world warms, patterns of rainfall are changing across the world.

So the whole world gets wetter?

Not exactly. Due to complex ocean currents and weather patterns, what's likely to happen is that more water will evaporate from already dry regions (drying them out even further), and be dumped on others that already receive heavy rainfall – causing heavy rains and floods. So many of the driest regions of the world will get even drier, while the wettest get even wetter. Hence, the wettest places won't be great to live in either. To top it all off, the increased evaporation may also feed bigger tropical storms and hurricanes. And other problems – like waterborne diseases – may hit countries affected by flooding.

Will there be *anywhere* nice left to live?

Well for a while at least, large parts of Canada, North America, Northern Europe and Russia may do quite well. The freezing northern winters will ease up, many crops will grow better and there's plenty of high ground to build on to escape flooding. That said, in future, the dangerous summer heatwaves in Europe may get even worse. And as temperatures rise, wildfires are expected to destroy more

and more forests and homes in Russia, western Canada and the US every year.

What do we do? Where should we go?

The best thing would be to try and stop the climate change happening in the first place, rather than try to run away from it. Since all the world's countries depend on each other, we'll all be affected somehow.

Shouldn't we all work together to sort it out, then?

Sounds like a plan. I'm with ya. And, thankfully, so are the governments of most countries around the world. In 1992, they all got together to try to form the United Nations Convention on Climate Change (UNCCC), and promised to do two things. Number one – to try and figure out the climate change problem. Number two – to try and do something about it. Since then, they've created an international team of scientists who have produced reports every year on how bad the problem is. They've written the Kyoto Protocol, which was a promise between most of the UNCCC countries to cut greenhouse gas emissions. And they're currently trying to figure out what's best to do next.*

Is it working?

Well, yes and no. On the one hand, we know much more about climate change than we did before the UNCCC was formed, and many countries have managed to cut their greenhouse gas emissions – some of them by 40% or more. On the other hand, not everybody signed up to

* For more on international efforts to combat climate change, see *What are we doing about it all?* (page 69).

the Kyoto agreement, and some countries – like Australia, China and the US – have been steadily increasing their emissions, instead of cutting them.

That doesn't sound very fair. Don't they know they're messing up the world for everyone else?

Well, it's not quite as simple as that. It's much easier for some countries to cut emissions than others. Huge countries like the US and China, for example, have massive populations (about 390 million for the US, and 1.3 *billion* for China). So even if each person is creating only a small amount of greenhouse gas per day, multiplied by hundreds of millions of people, that adds up to a lot. And to feed, house and supply all those people with what they need takes many more farms, buildings, factories and vehicles than you find in smaller countries. So this, too, ramps up their emissions.

But they have to do *something*, right? I mean, if they just keep putting it off, then all those floods and droughts and heatwaves and fires and stuff will mess their countries up anyway.

True. It's a tough one. They just have to keep talking and cooperating until they can figure out the best way through the problem for everybody.

Hope they figure it out soon, while the world's still a nice place to live in.

Me too. I kind of like living in the world. And there's nowhere else to live . . .

On the Move

Within the history of human technology and invention, some machines are so important that they changed our entire way of life – the clock, the printing press, the telephone – without them the modern world we know and love would be quite a different place.

But let's face it – the coolest machines in the world are the ones that let us zoom all over the planet at crazy, breakneck speeds. Cars, trains, ships and planes carry us across countries, across continents and across oceans. And they do it all in style.

So lots of questions, then, from all you speed-freaks out there. How do ships float, planes fly and rockets tear through the atmosphere? How will they change in the future? How big will they get? How will we power them? Will they drive themselves?

And of course – most importantly ...

> You got a question from:
> **Name:** Rikesh
> **Question:** If you travel at the speed of sound, and you fart, would you smell the fart before you hear it?

So let's tear it up with a high-speed tour through the world of transport technology.

And for Rikesh – that depends how loud the engine is, and whether the window is open ...

Why don't big metal ships just sink?

As long as a ship weighs less than the amount of water it pushes aside, it'll float. And since massive volumes of water can weigh thousands of tonnes – big metal ships can too.

Hang on — that doesn't make any sense. If you lob a feather into a pond, it'll float. But if you lob a coin in, it'll sink — right?

Right. But why does it sink?

Because it's made of metal. So it's heavier.

So what about an empty cola can? What if you threw that into a pond?

I wouldn't do that. I'm environmentally friendly, me.

OK, fine – into your bath, then. Just as an experiment.

Well, it would . . . float, I s'pose.

Right – it would. But the can's made of metal too (usually aluminum, these days). So why do cans float but not coins?

Cos coins are heavier?

Nope – I'm afraid not. Most coins weigh between 4g and 12g, and the average aluminium can weighs about 14g. A single pound coin and an empty cola can weigh roughly the same (the can is a little heavier). So other than weight, what's the difference between an empty can and a coin?

The can is bigger. And it's hollow?

Right – now we're getting somewhere. It's not just the weight, but the size (or volume) that's important. Over 2,000 years ago, a clever Greek mathematician called Archimedes figured this out while playing about in the bath. The story goes that he once hopped into an over-filled bath, causing water to flow over the sides. Rather than mop it up and drain a bit out, he filled the bath right up and experimented with submerging objects of different sizes into it, and collecting the water that overflowed each time.

Weird guy.

Fair point. But through his playful bathtime experiments, he quickly realized that the amount of water on the floor was equal to the amount of space taken up by (or the *volume* of) the objects he pushed into the bath. Each object pushed out (or *displaced*) a volume of water equal to itself.

Duhhh! That's not so clever.

Wait for it – here's the clever bit. Eventually, he also realized that if the object weighed less than the amount of water it displaced, then it floated. If it weighed more, then it sank. And that's why the pound coin sinks but the empty can

doesn't – they both weigh about the same, but the big, hollow can displaces (or pushes aside) more water.

OK . . . got it. And that's all very well for cans and coins, but what about cruise ships and oil tankers and stuff. They're HUGE. They can't weigh less than water, can they?

If they shift enough of it, then yes. The weight of seawater varies (depending on how warm it is, among other things), but on average it's roughly 1 tonne per cubic metre.

Now, the *Queen Mary 2* is one of the biggest cruise liners in the world. It's over 345m long, and at 72m high it's taller than a twenty-one-storey building. Dropped into the ocean, the hull of this massive steel ship pushes aside about 76,000 tonnes of seawater to make room for itself. Since the ship weighs less than this – even with nearly 4,000 people on board – it happily stays afloat in the Atlantic Ocean as it sails between the UK and the USA.

All right, then — what about oil tankers?

Their wide, flat shape helps push even more water aside, and allows for even heavier loads. The largest in the world is a Norwegian supertanker called the *Knock Nevis*. It's 458m long, 69m wide, and the bottom of its hull sits 25m below the surface of the water. Multiply those together, and you'll see that it displaces about 780,000 cubic metres of water, which would weigh roughly 790,000 tonnes. Fully loaded with 4 million barrels of oil, the *Knock Nevis* 'only' weighs 650,000 tonnes. So once again, the water weighs more than the ship . . .

. . . and it floats.

Exactly.

So there's no limit to how big you can build a ship?

Well, making them float is one thing – shifting them through the water is another. It's still not easy to get a 650,000 tonne oil tanker moving. But with light enough materials, and big enough engines, the sky (or rather the sea) is the limit. One company even wants to build a mile-long 'Freedom Ship' housing an entire city full of people. This floating civilization would have most of everything it needs to support itself on board, and would take years to sail the globe. But it hasn't been built yet, and many people doubt it ever will be. Still – a floating country might come in handy if climate change raises the sea levels enough.

Hmmm — all the same, I think I'll stay where I am.

Why's that?

I kind of like not worrying about whether or not my country's going to spring a leak.

How big can an aeroplane get before it's too heavy to fly?

In theory, there's almost no limit to how big a plane could get. But building, flying and handling super-giant aeroplanes create their own problems for air travel. So, if we made them too big, they just wouldn't be very useful.

So we could make super-huge planes — like, much bigger than jumbo jets — and they'd still fly?

We have already, and yes – they do. The Airbus A380 'Superjumbo' entered service for Singapore Airlines in 2007. The A380 is 73m long, and has an 80m wingspan. It can carry up to 850 passengers – 50% more than an average jumbo jet – and, fully loaded, it weighs almost 590,000kg (590 tonnes). Despite this, it can cruise happily at up to 43,000ft at a speed of around 650mph.

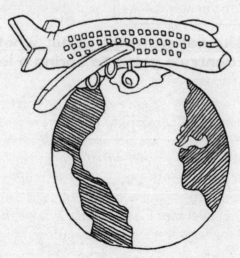

Yikes! Is that the biggest?

Almost. The Russian AN-225 Mriya (or 'Dream') transport plane is even bigger, at 84m long and 88m across the wings. It was built to carry rocket parts for the Russian Space programme, and currently holds the heavyweight aeroplane flight record, after lifting over 600,000kg (600 tonnes) to 6,500ft in 1989.

But how does something that heavy even get up into the air, let alone stay there? I know they do, but it just doesn't seem right.

What do you mean?

I mean, little planes and gliders are only light, so it shouldn't be that hard to get them off the ground. But how do you get something the size of a house into the air and keep it there?

Well, with big enough wings and engines, you can get more or less anything airborne. Even a house. That said, a house wouldn't handle too well in the air, and most houses would fall apart in the attempt. But it's not the weight or size of the house that would stop you doing it.

Why's that, then?

It's all to do with the science of flight – what physicists call *aerodynamics*. There are four basic forces acting on a flying aeroplane (or an airborne house, flying bus or whatever). These are *gravity*, *lift*, *thrust* and *drag*.

Gravity is the simple one – it just pulls the plane towards the Earth. All else being equal, the more massive the plane, the more it's weighed down by the force of gravity, and the harder it is to get it in the air.

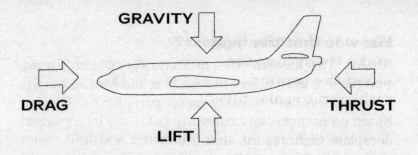

GRAVITY

DRAG

THRUST

LIFT

Right! Exactly! So how . . .

. . . hang on a minute – we're not done yet.

Oh – OK.

To overcome the pull of gravity, you have to counteract it by creating *lift*. Lift pulls (or rather pushes) the plane upwards, away from the Earth, and if you can generate enough of it you can get even the heaviest objects into the sky. One way to do this is with a big, horizontal propeller or rotor – as helicopters do. These have angled blades that push air downwards at high pressure, propelling the aircraft in the opposite direction – straight up. Aeroplanes, though, do it differently.

How's that?

Well, aeroplane engines (whether propeller or jet engines) push air backwards, propelling them forwards. This forward motion is called *thrust*. As the plane pushes through the air, it also creates *drag*. This force is caused by friction between the plane and the air rubbing against it, and pulls the plane backwards, slowing it down. To get off the ground, the thrust has to be powerful enough to overcome the drag, allowing the plane to accelerate to take-off speed.

But wouldn't that just make them thunder along the ground, rather than take off?

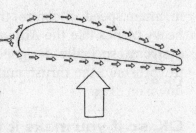

Right. The thrust itself does not generate lift. But it does create enough air flow around the wings to help *them* generate the lift the plane needs. Wings basically turn, or deflect, the backward-rushing flow of air downwards, which pushes the wing itself upwards, producing lift. The curved shape of the wing helps with this, but it's not as important as the size of the wing or the angle at which it cuts through the air (a flat wing at the correct angle will produce lift, but a curved wing at the wrong angle will not). So if the *thrust* is big enough to overcome the *drag*, then the *lift* generated may be big enough to overcome *gravity* and get the plane into the air – at least temporarily. Got it?

Got it. So why can't you just put wings and engines on your house, and fly it around the world? That way you wouldn't have to pay for hotels and stuff when you get there . . .

That's a marvellous idea – and I for one would love to fly my house to the Caribbean – but unfortunately it just isn't very practical. Most houses are built to stand, silent and still, for many years on hard ground. And while it is possible to overcome their weight with big enough engines and wings and power them towards take-off, the force of the thrust needed would most likely rip them to pieces. And, even if you got them airborne, the drag created by their rough, square-edged structures would make it difficult to maintain speed, or control their direction in the air. Huge, heavy planes like the Airbus A380 get around this using a strong, specially designed *airframe* – strong enough to withstand the thrust, and streamlined in shape to cut down on drag.

OK, so if you make it the right shape and it's strong enough, it doesn't matter how heavy the plane is. So why don't we have planes even bigger and heavier than those we have already?

Partly because we haven't built aeroplane engines powerful enough to get anything heavier than the Superjumbo or AN-225 to take-off speed. Also, the heavier the plane, the more massive the wing size needed to generate lift. This, in turn, adds *more* weight, meaning we need ever stronger (yet lighter) materials to build them. And, even if you can *build* them, that doesn't mean you can *use* them.

What do you mean?

Well, in general, the heavier the plane, the higher the take-off speed needed to get it airborne. And while powerful engines can manage this, it doesn't happen all at once. In fact, the more massive the plane, the slower it accelerates, meaning you need a longer runway for take-off and landing. Most airports don't have long enough runways to cope with the Airbus Superjumbo, and the few that can have had to extend their runways or build new ones. A conventional plane two or three times heavier than that would need such a ridiculously long runway that it would be driving most of the way towards its destination along the ground! Because of this, the future of heavyweight flight may lie with jets, airships or rockets* that can take off and land vertically. But we're still a little way off using those for everyday travel and transport.

So the sky might be full of high-tech rockets and airships one day? Like in all those 'future' movies?

Could be.

Hmmm — large, floating airships getting buzzed by big, pointy rockets . . . that sounds a bit dodgy to me.

Good point. You can have the airship, then. I'll be in the rocket.

Hey — no fair!

Sci-facts: five things that weigh roughly the same as the AN-225 Mriya aeroplane

1.3 million soccer balls

8,800 people

130 African elephants

46 fire engines

3.3 jumbo jets

---

* For more about the future of rocket flight, see *Will rockets replace aeroplanes one day?* (page 137).

Why don't aeroplanes fly in straight lines between airports?

They can't, because that would mean flying straight through the Earth itself. On the other hand, they *kind of do* follow straight lines – it just doesn't look that way on a flat map of the world.

Hang on a minute — planes can fly in any direction they want to, right?

Right – if they're allowed to.

And they don't have to follow roads or rivers, or fly around mountains or anything?

Nope. Not the big passenger planes, anyway. They can fly over any mountain on the planet. Jumbo jets usually cruise at an altitude of around 37,000ft. Everest – the world's highest mountain – is only about 29,000ft high.

So I don't get it. I mean, when you look at an airline map, the paths curve all over the place. If they can fly over anything, and the shortest distance between two places is a straight line, then why don't they fly straight?

Because that would only work if the world was flat, like the map itself. Over a flat surface, you're right – the shortest distance between two points (call them A and B) would be a straight line. But if A and B are on different sides of a solid object you can't move through, then you've got a problem. You have to go around, rather than through –

following the shortest path across the surface of the object. In this case, the shortest path takes us around the curved surface of the Earth, rather than straight through the middle of it in some sort of flying-tunnelling machine.

That *would* be cool though, wouldn't it?

Yes, it would. Very cool.

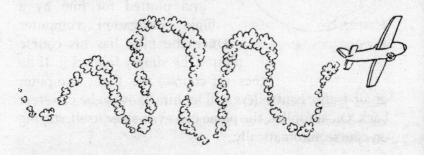

Just think — it'd be like: Nyyeeeeeeeeowwwww! Whoosh! Dive! Dive! Wham! Digga-digga-digga-digga . . .

Ri-ight . . . but since we can't do that we have to settle for flying our regular, non-tunnelling planes in arcs, following the curving surface of the Earth below. When you plot that on a flattened-out map of the world, it looks like the line between the origin and destination airports has been bent upwards or downwards to form a curve. But this is only because the map is flat, or two-dimensional. On a spherical, three-dimensional map – such as a globe or a 3D computer simulation map – you'd see the plane was actually flying pretty much straight.

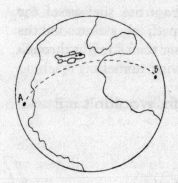

But how does the pilot decide which curve to follow, or how far to swerve out?

Well spotted. Actually, he (or she) doesn't decide – the curved course is calculated and plotted for him by a flight navigation computer. Once the pilot has his course plotted, he simply follows it. If he goes off-course, the flight computer or air-traffic controllers will let him know so he can steer back. On autopilot, the plane can even steer itself, staying on course automatically.

All right, then how does the computer figure out which curve to use?

The shortest distance between two points on the globe always follows part of a *great circle*, which is a huge circle going right round the globe with the centre of the Earth as its centre. The equator is a great circle – encircling the Earth horizontally. The path from the North to the South Pole and back again forms another (vertical) great circle, and there are any number of other great circles at all the angles in between. To find the shortest distance, the computer finds a great circle with both airports on its circumference and the centre of the Earth as its centre. The arc (or part of the circle) between the airports is called a *geodesic*, and it's this curved path that the plane follows.

This can look a little strange on a standard map. For example, the straight path from London to Sydney on a flat map goes through France, Italy and Saudi Arabia, eventually approaching Australia from the west. But the geodesic path actually followed by airlines curves 'upward' through Denmark, Russia, China and Indonesia, approaching Australia from the north, almost.

Weird. So flights always follow these great circle things, then?

Not exactly. The great circles give the *shortest* possible path, but that doesn't mean it's always the quickest or safest. The course might have to go around no-fly zones in some countries and cities. Or the pilot might decide to curve out further to the north or south to catch a tail wind, getting him there faster. And, closer to the airports, air-traffic controllers might steer them away from the direct route to avoid coming too close to other aircraft.*

Is that why they always circle around for ages before landing? So they don't hit other planes?

That, and to put themselves at the right angle to approach a runway. Since aircraft can approach the airport from any direction – but the runways only run in a few directions – each plane has to circle around until it's lined up with a runway. Then it can approach slowly from a distance and safely put down.

Why can't they just hit the brakes, dive at the runway and level off at the last minute? I think I saw that in a movie once . . .

Well, some small planes can do this, but I wouldn't try it in a passenger jet. Planes have to stay above a minimum

---

* For more about flight speeds, see *If the Earth spins eastwards, how come westward flights aren't way quicker than eastward ones?* (page 128).

speed to stay in the air, and the bigger the plane, the higher the speed.* Also, if they dive too steeply, they'll have trouble controlling their speed and stopping the momentum of the dive. For this reason, most pilots (sensibly) approach the runway from a distance, slowing down and decreasing altitude gradually until they gently touch down.

So the plane takes off, flies in a great circle curve — which is really a straight line — then circles around until it can land straight . . . right?

Exactly.

I'm glad we got that straight.

Or curved.

Gahh — stop it!

Sorry.

---

* For more about how aeroplanes stay in the air, see *How big can an aeroplane get before it's too heavy to fly?* (page 116).

Practical science: make your own flight path

Want to see how geodesic arcs work for real? Then try this:

1 Grab an orange. Any one will do, but try to get one with a fairly smooth skin. This is your planet Earth.

2 Get two pins and stick them into the orange at any two points around its surface. Be careful not to stab a finger, and watch out for squirty juice in the eye (which will be funny for everyone except you).

3 Now get a piece of string or a shoelace and tie it between the two pins, forming a line.

4 With a biro or felt-tip pen, trace along the line to draw your flight path.

5 Now take out the pins, remove the string, and carefully peel the orange – making sure not to tear the skin across your flight-path line.

6 Now flatten out the skin on a table. Is the line now straight, or curved?

7 Congratulations – you've made a geodesic flight path. Perhaps for a tiny insect pilot.

8 You may now eat the planet.

If the Earth spins eastwards, how come westward flights aren't way quicker than eastward ones?

Because the Earth's atmosphere and all the aeroplanes flying in it spin eastwards too – cancelling out the planet's motion. In fact, due to headwinds and tailwinds, flights west are often much *slower* than flights east.

Spinning aeroplanes?! Wouldn't they make you throw up?

Well, they're not really spinning – they're just travelling alongside the spin of the Earth. And, just as you can't feel the Earth turning beneath you as you stand on it, there's no 'spinning' sensation on the plane to make you sick.

You've lost me there.

OK, let's think about it for a minute. Right now, you're sitting, standing or lying down (depending on how you like to get comfortable when you're reading), and you're not moving or travelling anywhere. You're completely still. Right?

Right.

Wrong. Unless you're right at the North or South Pole (and, if so, I apologize), then you're sitting, standing or lying on a spot that is already moving. The spot you now occupy is currently circling the centre of the Earth once per day as the planet rotates on its axis. If you're at the equator – say, in Singapore, Kenya or Ecuador – then your 24-hour lap around the planet covers a distance of 25,000 miles, giving you a speed of over 1,000 miles per hour! As you go further north or south of the equator (which is the fattest part of the planet, creating the longest journey around) you don't need to travel so far, so your speed is a bit less. But the fact remains – even though you feel like you're sitting still, you're actually whipping around the centre of the planet at a dizzying pace.

So why can't you feel it?

In short, because you're moving at a constant speed, and there's nothing whipping by the other way to make you realize you're moving at all. It's a bit like being on a moving train. As long as the train isn't speeding up or slowing down, you can sit, stand, walk around and generally forget you're moving at all. Until, that is, you look out of the window and see trees and houses whipping by, or open a window and feel the rush of moving air.

When you're standing still, the trees, houses and air around you are held to the surface of the Earth by the same force you are – gravity. So, while it feels like you and your surroundings are motionless, they're actually travelling along with you in your journey around the globe – all whipping along at the same speed. Physicists call this idea *relative motion*. It's only useful to say you're travelling at a certain speed *relative*, or *in relation to*, something else. So, when we're sitting still, we have *zero speed* or *motion* in relation to the Earth beneath us, and we can happily ignore the fact that we're all, in fact, moving.

OK, but how does that work with aeroplanes and flying things? I mean, if you take off in a plane or a helicopter, you're not on the Earth any more,

right? So, if the Earth is turning so fast, couldn't you just hover above Europe in a helicopter for a few hours until America rolled beneath you?

Nice idea, but it wouldn't work, I'm afraid.

Why not?

Because if the helicopter was truly hovering (rather than flying north, south, east or west), then it would be keeping itself motionless relative to the Earth beneath it and the atmosphere around it. Since we already know these are moving eastwards at up to 1,000mph, that means the helicopter will be doing the same. Seven hours later, it would still be hovering over Europe (provided it hadn't run out of fuel already).

Gahh!! Fine! What about flying *towards* America in an aeroplane, then? If America is rolling eastwards, and you're flying westwards, then America and your plane are moving towards each other, so it should be way quicker getting there, right?

I'm afraid not.

But why not?!

Because, if you think about it, even before your plane took off – sitting stationary on the runway – it was travelling eastwards at high speed, along with the rest of Europe. Let's say it takes off and heads west at 300mph. That 300mph is measured in relation to the European airport it took off from, to the American one it's headed towards, and to the atmosphere over the Atlantic Ocean it has to fly through. But since both airports and the air between them are also rotating eastwards at well over 300mph, that means the plane is still, technically, moving eastwards – just 300mph slower than the airports and atmosphere!

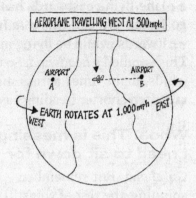

If that sounds too confusing (and it does to me!), then you can use relative motion to ignore the fact that the plane, the airports and the atmosphere are rotating with the Earth, and think about it this way: when a plane is sitting on the runway, it has *zero speed* relative to the airport. After take-off, it's moving towards the American airport at a *relative speed* of 300mph. And that's it. Since the 300mph speed is measured *relative to the airport*, it doesn't matter whether the airport is stationary or moving eastwards. All that matters is that the plane is covering the distance between the two airports at 300mph. It takes six to ten hours to get there because that's how long it takes to travel that distance. End of story.

So flights take the same time going east or west, then?

Not quite. The times can differ, but this is due to wind patterns within the atmosphere, rather than the turning of the Earth. For example, the winds over the Atlantic between America and Europe generally blow strongest west to east (especially at higher altitudes, where they form a high-speed air current called the 'jet stream'). So a plane flying eastwards has the wind behind it and will go faster. We call this a *tailwind*. The same plane flying westwards would be flying into the wind, slowing it down. This is called a *headwind*. So thanks to headwinds and tailwinds, flight times across many well-travelled air routes are often shorter heading east than they are heading west.

Whoa. This is messing with my head. I think I need to sit down for while.

Go ahead. But remember – even when your head stops spinning, the rest of you still will be.

Not helping, dude.

Sorry.

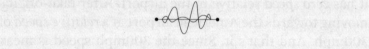

Why can't aeroplanes fly into Space?

Because aeroplanes need air pressure to fly, and there ain't too much of that up in Space . . .

What's air pressure got do with it? I mean, why can't the pilot just point the plane straight up and take a Space detour. That would rule.

Yes, it would. You could float around, weightless. You could see the whole Earth at once, as a big, blue ball. You could buzz satellites and Space stations . . .

Exactly!

. . . but unfortunately, a standard aeroplane could never do this. Aeroplanes need air pressure against their wings in order to fly, and outside of the Earth's atmosphere, there just isn't any.

But don't the engines make aeroplanes fly?

Well, yes and no. Jet or propeller engines provide the forward force – or thrust* – which pushes the aircraft through the air. But it's the wings that really lift an aeroplane and keep it in the air. They're flatter across the bottom surface, but curved across the top. This forces air molecules rushing over the top of each wing to travel a longer distance in order to reach the rear edge than those skimming across the bottom. This 'thins out' the air moving over the wing and drops the air pressure above it. So the high pressure below and low pressure above combine to lift the wing – and the aeroplane – upwards. Without air, though, none

---

* For more about how thrust works and how aeroplanes fly, see *How big can an aeroplane get before it's too heavy to fly?* (page 116).

of this works. With no rushing air to deflect, there's no lift, and the plane can no longer fly.

Couldn't they fly up to the *edge* of Space, at least? Like where the atmosphere ends and Space begins?

Not really, since the atmosphere doesn't really have an 'edge' – it just thins out gradually and blends into airless Space.

What do you mean?

When they talk about the atmosphere, scientists divide it into five layers, based on how far up it goes, how warm or cold it is and other features. The lowest layer is called the *troposphere*. It stretches from the ground to between 4–12 miles above the Earth (it's thinner at the poles and thickest at the equator). This is the layer we live in, and that almost all aircraft fly in.

Above that, you have the *stratosphere*, which extends up to 30 miles above the surface. Above that, you've

got the *mesosphere* (up to 50 miles), the *thermosphere* (370 miles) and finally the *exosphere*, which extends over 6,000 miles into Space. Space shuttles orbit in the thermosphere. Satellites orbit in the exosphere. But the highest an aeroplane has ever gone is 96,500ft, or 18 miles, into the stratosphere. And that was an unmanned high-altitude plane built by NASA, specially designed to fly in air a hundred times thinner than at ground level.

All right, so if planes can't fly that high, how do rockets manage it?

They use rocket engines, which work differently to aeroplane ones, and don't depend on air around the craft to make it move. Instead, they use solid or liquid fuels – plus oxygen – packed inside the rocket's fuel tanks. The fuels are mixed and exploded inside the engine, and the hot exhaust gases rush out of the back of the rocket through a nozzle, propelling the craft in the opposite direction. If the engine's pointing backwards, the rocket goes forwards. At lift-off, the engines point downwards, so the rocket goes upwards.

What if you put rocket engines on an aeroplane — *then* could it get up there?

Yes, it could. And, in fact, this has already been done. Just recently, two-staged Spaceplanes have been designed to take tourists 62 miles up, into the thermosphere, for a taste of Space travel. These have standard aeroplane jet engines on their first stage and methane-powered rocket engines on their second – the stage that takes the crew up *really* high before gliding back to Earth.

Spaceplanes?! How cool is that?!

Very.

Even the word is cool. *Spaceplane*.
Spaaace Plaaannne. Suh-pace-puh-lane . . .

Right.

So when can I go?

Well, that depends. The first regular Spaceplane service should be up and running by 2012, but it might cost you a bit.

How much?

150,000 pounds. At least.

Uhhhhhh . . .

Better get saving!

Sci-facts: high-flying planes through history

Aircraft	Altitude reached	Year
Wright Flyer	10ft	1903
Bell X-1 'Glamorous Glennis' rocket plane	70,140ft	1947
X-15 rocket plane	354,000ft	1963
Spaceship One (rocket-powered Spaceplane)	367,000ft	2004

Will rockets replace aeroplanes one day?

Maybe, maybe not. Rocket-powered aeroplanes have been around for almost fifty years already, and may soon be carrying tourists to the edge of Space. But aeroplanes are still cheaper, safer and more useful than rockets for air travel and, as long as they stay that way, we won't be doing away with them.

What?! You mean rocket-powered planes have been around for ages?

Yup. The first rocket planes were invented in Europe during the 1940s and 1950s, during and after World War Two. The most successful – the US Air Force's X-15 rocket plane – set new airspeed records in the 1960s, and climbed to a record-breaking height of 350,067ft, or 67 miles, during test flights. Which, technically, made the pilot an astronaut.

So why aren't we using them?

Two reasons, really – they're not as good as regular rockets for Space travel, and they're not as good as regular aeroplanes for air travel. Which kind of makes them the piggy in the middle.

Yeah, but they're a *rocket-powered* piggy in the middle. So what's the problem? I mean, how can they not be as good as aeroplanes if they're so much faster?

Faster doesn't necessarily mean better. Currently, the fastest aircraft in the world is the Space Shuttle orbiter, which re-enters the atmosphere at over 17,500mph. But you can't exactly hop on one of those for a trip to Spain and back. Think about it – why not?

Because there's only one of them, and NASA are busy with it?

Well, sort of . . . NASA have actually built six shuttles in total, but they only use one at a time. So let's say they built a few more. Enough for one at every airport. Any problems now?

Errr . . . you'd still need a huge launch pad for lift-off?

Right – the Shuttle can't take off on its own, like a conventional aircraft. It has to be launched into Space using booster rockets and millions of litres of fuel. Which makes it rather expensive to fly.

. . . And you'd probably miss France and land in Antarctica or something anyway. Unless you did a lap of the world first . . .

Right. Rockets are great for getting into orbit, but are generally trickier to launch and a *lot* more expensive to run than aeroplanes. As for rocket planes, they don't carry enough fuel – and don't reach high enough speeds – to get into orbit, making them no good for Space travel.

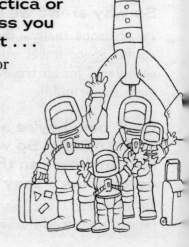

And they suffer from similar launch and cost problems as rockets, making them (for now at least) less useful than aeroplanes for air travel. Even the record-breaking X-15 rocket plane had to be flown into the high atmosphere by a carrier aeroplane before it could be launched. It could never have taken off by itself.

So now we're left with big, clunky jet planes to fly around in. Pah. B-o-r-ing.

Well, they're not that boring. As jet engines have improved, they've started to catch up with rocket speeds, anyway.* The airspeed record for a jet aircraft stands at about 2,200mph, which is about half the speed record set by the X-15 rocket plane in 1967. Plus passenger jets are getting bigger** and faster, and future airliners might even have movable engines, allowing them to take off and land vertically, like present-day military jump-jets. And besides – rocket planes aren't done for yet. Right now, several companies are racing to build rocket-powered Spaceplanes to take tourists on adventure flights to the edge of Space.

That sounds good. Tell me more.

The first private, reusable Spaceplane on the scene was built by American aerospace company Scaled Composites. Their test craft, SpaceShipOne, flew to an altitude of over 367,000ft, or 69.6 miles – breaking the X-15's altitude record. Like the X-15, SpaceShipOne had to be carried to high altitude before launch, attached to a specially built carrier plane called the White Knight. Sponsored by the

---

* For more about the difference between jet engines and rocket engines, see *Why can't aeroplanes fly into Space?* (page 133).

** For more about how big, heavy planes stay in the air, see *How big can an aeroplane get before it's too heavy to fly?* (page 116).

Virgin Group, they're now busy building SpaceShipTwo (complete with White Knight Two) and an entire spaceport in the Mojave Desert, in the south-western USA.

A spaceport? Cooooooool.

But that's not the only spaceplane in the works. Another, built by the European Aeronautic Defence and Space company (EADS) might be taking off and landing at normal airports by 2012. This one is basically a small jet plane with a rocket engine whacked on the back of it and half-filled with rocket fuel. It'll take off normally, climb to 39,000ft, then briefly kick in the rocket engine to blast itself to an altitude of 328,100ft, or 62 miles. Here, passengers will be able to unbuckle their seatbelts and drift around in zero gravity for about three minutes. They'll also be able to view the Earth below through portholes all around the cabin. Then they strap back in, and the plane re-enters the atmosphere and lands at an airport as normal.

That's it — I wanna go.

You and about 15,000 people a year, it's reckoned.

Yeah, but I'm going *first*.

And it won't be cheap.

Don't care — still going.

All right, then – race ya to the spaceport!

Hey! Come back!

If rockets 'burn up' in the atmosphere, why don't we?

Because, unlike rockets re-entering the atmosphere, we're already *in it*. Plus we're moving along with the atmosphere, so we don't have to worry about rubbing it the wrong way . . .

What do you mean, 'we're already in it'? I thought rockets came through the atmosphere to get back to Earth . . .

They do. But they don't come through it and out the other side. The atmosphere isn't like a shell the rocket has to crack through – it's a layer of gases that extends out into Space, but also goes all the way down to the ground. In fact, that's kind of where it begins.*

How's that?

The Earth's atmosphere is just a massive cloud of air (consisting of nitrogen, oxygen and smaller amounts of other gases) held close to the Earth by its gravitational pull. We live in the bit at the surface, where the air is thickest. But the further away from the Earth you get, the weaker the effect of its gravity. So the higher up (or rather, further out) you go, the thinner the atmosphere becomes. When a spacecraft is launched into orbit, it leaves the atmosphere – or at least gets so far out that there's hardly any of it. The problem comes when it's time to return to Earth, as this means re-entering the atmosphere. Done wrong, this can cause the spacecraft to burn up or rip itself to pieces.

---

* For more about the atmosphere, see *Why can't aeroplanes fly into Space?* (page 133).

Still don't get it. You're saying we live in the atmosphere, and we're fine . . .

Right.

. . . but if rockets try to come in — and do it wrong — then they can explode. So why doesn't the atmosphere make *us* explode?

Because it's not the atmosphere itself that heats up and damages the spacecraft. It's the friction and strain caused by the spacecraft ploughing into the atmosphere at high speed and rubbing against it. So it's the difference in speed that makes the meeting between the spacecraft and the atmosphere a dangerous business. Since we're already in the atmosphere – and stuck to the surface of the Earth along with it – we're moving at the same speed it is, and there's no friction. Not so for a spacecraft.

A Space Shuttle, for example, has to maintain a speed of around 4.8 miles per second, or 17,300mph, just to stay in orbit. That's over eight times faster than a bullet speeding from a high-powered rifle. So, when the spacecraft comes out of orbit and contacts the atmosphere, it hits it at enormous speed and generates massive amounts of friction as it punches through the air. This is what heats the craft up.

So if it's moving too fast, why doesn't the pilot just slow it down in Space, then come back down safely, without all the friction and heat and stuff?

Unfortunately, that would take more fuel than the Shuttle could carry up there in the first place. It takes around a million litres of fuel just to boost the Shuttle into orbit, and once the fuel is used up the heavy boosters and fuel tanks that carry it drop off to make the craft lighter. The Shuttle can only carry a little more fuel for its return journey. So instead of blasting its way back to a safe speed for descent, it turns around, burns a little fuel and slows down just enough to take itself out of orbit and begin 'falling' back towards the Earth. Then, as the Shuttle re-enters the atmosphere, it actually *uses* the friction it generates to slow itself down. This friction converts massive amounts of its speed and movement (or kinetic energy) into heat, and the underside of the spacecraft glows red hot as it re-enters the atmosphere.

I've seen that on the telly. But why don't rockets melt when they do that?

Some of them *do* melt, as it happens. On purpose.

What?!

Since the Shuttle and other spacecraft need the friction to slow themselves, they can't avoid getting hot. So some re-entry craft (such as those used by the Russian, Chinese and European Space programmes) are built with a thick layer on the bottom called an ablation shield. This is designed to melt away a little at a time as the craft re-enters. The gradually melting shield then buys enough time for the craft to slow down to a speed safe enough to open a parachute. The Space Shuttle, on the other hand, uses heat-resistant tiles to shield its underside, which can be replaced for future missions.

So what happens then?

Well, if all goes well, the Shuttle slows to a couple of hundred miles an hour, and glides into a safe landing much like a normal aeroplane – except that it's moving quite a bit faster – so it releases parachutes to quickly slow itself after touching down.

Sounds like a pretty wild ride. What's it like?

During re-entry, there would be a deafening roar of fiery air all around the craft, and the whole cabin would shudder and kick about, racked by huge g-forces for about thirty minutes. So it'd probably be like the scariest theme-park ride you've ever been on. Times a hundred.

Times infinity, more like!

And the launch wouldn't be too different. Noise, fire, g-forces . . . the works. That's one reason why astronauts and cosmonauts have to train for months or years – to withstand the mental and physical stress.

Wow — imagine you were the first one to try that out. That dude must have been pretty brave. Or pretty crazy . . .

Maybe he was a little of both! Yuri Gagarin was the young Russian cosmonaut who, on 12 April 1961, first braved all this stuff to become the first man in Space. As a military test pilot he was used to flying experimental aircraft at crazy speeds. But, for his first space flight, his training involved sitting in a whirling centrifuge to experience huge g-forces, and being in a room with no sound or light for twenty-four hours to get used to the dark, cramped conditions of the re-entry capsule. As his Vostok rocket roared into its fiery launch, he actually cheered '*Poyekhali!*', which means 'Here we go!', into his headset.

I probably would've said something more like 'YAAAAAGGGHHH!!!' Or whatever that is in Russian.

I think it's still 'YAAAAAGGGHHH'.

Oh — right. It would've been pretty scary, anyway — knowing that you were the first one to go, and not knowing if you'd make it back.

Actually, before Gagarin went up, there were plenty of non-human astronauts and cosmonauts launched into Space – just to check if a human could survive at all. So the first earthlings in Space were actually mice, dogs, monkeys, chimps and fruit flies.

That must have been difficult.

How d'you mean?

Well, you know, getting a fruit fly into a spacesuit and all.

What?!

I mean, that must've been one *tiny* helmet . . .

If normal car engines cause pollution, why don't we all use electric ones?

Because electric engines still suffer from a few drawbacks, and if you have to charge the battery with energy from fossil fuels, then you're still creating pollution. So while electric and part-electric cars are less damaging to the environment, they can't solve the whole pollution problem on their own.

Drawbacks? But petrol cars have drawbacks too, right?

True, they do. Cars burning oil-based petrol (or gasoline) as fuel release nitrous oxides and other harmful pollutants, which can react with ozone and sunlight to form photochemical smog. Smog clouds form dark, stinky, hazy layers over traffic-laden cities, causing health problems for people that live there. Petrol engines also release large amounts of carbon dioxide, which enters the atmosphere and acts as a greenhouse gas, trapping heat and warming the Earth as part of the global-warming process.*

There you go, then. So electric cars might have drawbacks, but they can't be as bad as all that, can they? All we have to do is stick batteries and electric motors in our cars instead of engines, and the problem's sorted.

Well, not quite. It's true that electric motors can run without producing exhaust fumes – which avoids all the

---

* For more about the greenhouse effect, see *Can we really stop the greenhouse effect and global warming?* (page 74).

problems above. But batteries alone won't sort the problem out, I'm afraid.

Why's that?

For starters, cars are big, power-hungry machines, and they need a lot more power than your calculator or laptop. So if you're running one on electricity alone, you need a lot of batteries. Big, heavy batteries can weigh the car down, and limit how fast it can speed up. A tankful of petrol contains much more energy than a series of chemical batteries of the same weight. So petrol cars can go faster and run further than electric cars on the same weight of fuel. This not only makes electric cars less powerful but it also means you have to refuel (recharge) them more often than petrol cars to keep them running.

Yeah, but who cares? So you have to go a bit slower, and they're not quite so powerful. Boo hoo.

Then there's the inconvenience of refuelling. Batteries can't be charged while you're driving – you have to take them home and plug them in. It can take several hours to recharge the whole lot.

So you have to remember to plug them in at night. Big deal. No fumes! No global warming!

No fumes, perhaps. But batteries still can't get around the global warming problem.

Eh? Why not?

Think about it for a minute – when you recharge the battery, where does the power come from?

Erm . . . power stations.

Right. Which burn coal, gas or oil to produce the electricity in the first place. So, while you might not be burning fossil fuels in your car, it's only because they've already been burned for you, somewhere else.

What about nuclear power stations?

They don't burn fossil fuels, but they do create hazardous nuclear waste. So they're a bit better, but not much. And it'll probably stay that way until we figure out how to dispose of nuclear waste safely.

What about wind power, or solar power?

Ah – now you're getting somewhere. That would be the ideal solution, but right now we get less than 6% of our energy from renewable sources like wind, solar and hydro-electric power. Until that changes, we're stuck with burning fossil fuels for electricity, and electric cars can't enjoy any real advantage over petrol ones. That means even environmentally friendly people will be unlikely to buy them.

Some countries, like Iceland, are lucky enough to have

huge reserves of renewable energy right beneath them. Iceland gets over 99% of its energy from renewable sources, and the government there is planning to use these to create hydrogen fuels to power vehicles. Thanks to this, Iceland may be the first country in the world to have all of its cars, buses, boats and trains powered by renewable sources. For most countries, though, petrol cars are likely to hang around for some time yet. At least until the fossil fuels start running out. When that happens, everyone will have to start looking at other ways of powering their vehicles – whether they like it or not.

But won't all those petrol cars be doing loads of polluting between now and then?

Yup. Unfortunately.

Isn't there anything we can do in the meantime?

Maybe. While we might not be able to (or might not want to) switch straight over to all-electric cars, there might be an in-between option that helps us cut our exhaust gas emissions by using less petrol. A hybrid car.

Hybrid car? That sounds cool. Is that like two mutant alien cars all mangled together to create one, superpowered . . .

Err – no. It's a car with both a petrol engine and an electric motor. It can use both to power the wheels, and recycles energy from the movement of the car to recharge its own batteries. This means it performs as well as a petrol car, but burns less fuel, releases less harmful emissions and is friendlier to the environment.

Right. I knew that.

Since hybrid cars still use petrol, they're not the final answer to the problem. But they might be a stepping stone to even more environmentally friendly petrol cars, and might help tide us over until we can ditch fossil fuels once and for all.

Can anybody have one?

If you can drive, and you've got the money, then yes. There are many hybrids available already, and they're getting more popular all the time. But if you really want to be a friend to the environment, you could go one better by buying something else.

What's that?

A new bike. No petrol, zero emissions and no need to worry about recharging. Just you, your legs and the open road. Well – the open bicycle lane, anyway.

Sci-facts: 'green' vehicles

Aside from electric cars, there are a whole range of eco-friendly alternatives to petrol cars – some of which are already available, while others are still being developed. But none of them are perfect, and all have their good and bad points.

Natural gas cars

Good: run on natural gas, which burns much cleaner than petrol (releasing carbon dioxide, but fewer other pollutants like nitrous oxides).

Bad: have to be refuelled at home, or at special fuelling stations.

Hybrid cars

Good: powered by a (petrol-powered) engine and a (battery-powered) electric motor which recharges itself while driving. This helps recover energy and makes hybrids more efficient than petrol cars.

Bad: still burn petrol, releasing carbon dioxide and pollutants (although less than standard petrol cars for the same distance driven).

Biodiesel cars

Good: use a diesel fuel made from plant vegetable oils, chip fat, recycled grease or other sources – often blended with standard diesel fuel. Biodiesel burns more efficiently than petrol, and releases fewer pollutants.

Bad: biodiesel isn't yet available everywhere to buy. Carbon dioxide and pollutants are released during the farming that produces the plants and animals (that the oils and fats come from) in the first place.

Fuel-cell cars
Good: driven by a fuel cell that creates energy by reacting hydrogen fuel with oxygen, releasing water vapour, but no carbon dioxide or harmful pollutants.

Bad: use electricity to create the reaction (giving the same problem as electric cars, if the electricity comes from fossil fuels), and producing the hydrogen fuel also takes energy and releases carbon dioxide and pollutants.

Bicycles
Good: driven by your body, which releases no pollutants other than farts and BO.

Bad: good for getting around town, but it takes a while to get between cities and countries this way. Also generally unsafe to pick up three friends and take them on the motorway.

Will cars ever drive themselves?

Some already can! Many cars use advanced guidance technology to avoid obstacles and traffic, and a new generation of self-driving cars will soon be upon us.

Cars are driving themselves *already*?! How? Where?

Test versions of robot cars built in Japan, Germany and the US have driven hundreds of miles on their own, using radar and specially designed road sensors to find their way – even through heavy traffic. More advanced self-driving cars are being developed in the UK to shuttle passengers at London's Heathrow airport and spectators for the 2012 Olympic Games. Some of these use advanced laser sensors and Artificial Intelligence (AI)-type technology to detect and steer themselves around obstacles. Since 2004, there's even been a race for self-driving cars in America, called the DARPA Grand Challenge, funded by the US military. There, driverless 'robot' cars built by university engineering teams race each other on off-road courses to win cash prizes for their builders.

Sweet! So you can just jump in one, kick back and let it take you anywhere?

Not quite, but close. Most of these self-driving (or autonomous) cars were test models or prototypes. And many still needed input from drivers every once in a while throughout their journeys. And while completely autonomous cars were used in the off-road Grand Challenge races, the technology is still being developed. So driverless cars aren't quite ready to be rolled out on to busy public roads just yet.

Boo. Why not?

Because in order to be safe enough for everyone to use, the engineers and car builders have to prove that a totally autonomous car can drive itself at least as safely as a human could. And that's not easy to do.

You mean, like not going the wrong way, or not running into the back of other cars?

Actually, that's the simple part. Many cars now have navigation computers that use the Global Positioning System (GPS) to plot their routes along roads and motorways. And many more have cruise control, which keeps the car at a constant speed on motorways without the driver having to use the accelerator or brake pedals to keep it there. Some cars even have adaptive cruise control, which uses radar signals to detect other cars in front of it on the road, and adjusts the car's speed automatically to keep at a safe distance. So, if you put all those together, you've already got a car that knows where to go, and can speed up and slow down all on its own, without any input from a human driver.

But what about steering? How would it know how to follow a curvy road, or know not to swerve right off it?

Lots of cars have electronically assisted power steering so that you hardly have to move the steering wheel before it turns the rest of the way itself. And some cars have a system called 'lane keeping assist', which keeps the car on the road – and in the right lane – automatically.

No way! How does that work?

The system uses special cameras and sensors to detect both the edges of the road and the lane dividers (or dotted lines) down the middle. When the car veers left or right, the sensors notice it because the lines and lane markers on the road will have shifted the other way. So they use the power steering motors to nudge the steering wheel gently back the other way, keeping the car in lane and safely on the road. Right now, this 'steering nudge' system just stops the human driver from steering off course. But it's a fairly simple leap from that to a car that steers itself between lanes and around corners on purpose.

So if you stick all that together . . .

. . . Then you've basically got a car that can happily plot its route, steer itself around the roads and speed up or slow down to keep its distance from other cars. And that's what some car builders are starting to do. General Motors has already built cars with a system called TrafficAssist, which uses lasers, sensors and computers to recognize road signs, lane markings, other cars and bends in the road. The whole thing should be able to drive itself at up to 60mph, in all kinds of traffic, without the driver doing very much at all.

Brilliant! That's it, then. What more do you need for a self-driving car?

Well, even with all these features and functions, you probably still won't be able to turn around in the driver's seat, ignore the road and chat to friends while the car does all the driving. The TrafficAssist system is designed to make driving more relaxing and less effort, rather than to replace the driver completely. And it's still not clear how good it would be at reacting quickly to trouble. Human drivers scan the road far ahead and anticipate problems using creative thought and imagination. If you spot a truck weaving between lanes on the road, for example, you might deduce that the driver is half asleep at the wheel and take more care when passing it just in case it veers into you. Computer autopilots can't really do this. They just react to what's happening immediately around them, as and when it happens. And by the time the car's lasers and sensors noticed the truck swerving towards it, it might be too late for the car to steer itself away.

Yikes. Sounds a bit scary when you put it that way.

That said, human drivers aren't perfect either. Although we might be able to think ahead and use better judgement than a computer system, that doesn't mean we always do. Human drivers tend to fix their eyes on one bit of the road at a time, and ignore what's happening in others. We can be distracted by chatting passengers, changing CD tracks, or mobile phone calls. So, as self-driving cars arrive over the next decade, we'll all have to ask ourselves: who's more likely to crash – me, or the computer?

In that case, I dunno if I'd trust a computer to drive for me after all.

Why's that?

My stupid computer crashes all the time!

Will we ever ride in floating trains and buses?

Floating trains are already here! The Chinese have been using one since 2002, and more levitating trains are on the way. But we might have to wait a while longer for floating buses ...

You're serious? Real floating trains? Trains that really, actually *float*?

Yup. Been around for a few decades, now. They're called Magnetic Levitation trains, or Maglev trains for short.

Excellent! How do they work?

They use special switchable magnets to lift the train off the track, to speed it up and to slow it down. One set of magnets is in the track, and a second is attached to the train itself. When the magnets are activated in sequence, this not only causes the train to float one or two centimetres above the track, but also pushes and pulls it along the track. This means that no wheels are needed to drive the train along (although some models use wheels at lower speeds before the Maglev devices kick in). And no wheels and no contact with the track means no grinding machinery or friction against the rails to slow the train down. Because of this, Maglev trains can accelerate to incredible speeds, and the ride is so smooth you can hardly feel it.

But wouldn't magnets make the train stick to the track?

Not if they're arranged and activated so that they repel each other. Ever had a go at playing with two old-fashioned horseshoe-shaped magnets? If you have, you'll know that the ends, or poles, of the magnet can either attract or repel the poles of others, depending on how you line them up. That's because each magnet has both a positive and a negative pole (or, if you like, a north and a south pole). Try to stick two of the same pole together (like two 'norths' or two 'souths') and they repel each other. Put one of each together (one 'north' and one 'south') and they attract. It's this magnetic attraction and repulsion that is used by Maglev trains to levitate and drive themselves. The repulsion between one set of magnets in the track and another on the underside of the train carriage lifts the train free of the track surface. Depending on the design, another two sets of magnets might also be used to centre the train and stop it flying off the track.

But if it's that simple, why didn't we just stick magnets on trains a long time ago?

Because in reality, it's not *quite* that simple. For starters, Maglev trains don't use permanent magnets, like the horseshoe ones we've been describing – or rather, they don't *just* use permanent magnets. If you lined the track and the underside of train with those, you might be able to get the train to repel the track and float. If you were lucky, or you arranged them very cleverly, you might even be able to keep it from slipping off the track to one side or the other. But, at best, the train would just sit there, unable to move. It would still need a push or a pull from something – like an engine and a set of wheels – to get going. Which kind of defeats the object.

So what do the real floating trains use, then?

They use superconducting electromagnets. Electromagnets are made by looping electrical wire around certain metals or ceramics, which creates a kind of switchable, temporary magnet. (In fact, all wires or cables carrying an electrical current are surrounded by magnetic fields, so coiling them up just concentrates the field, making the magnetic effect stronger.) This type of magnet only works when you run an electric current through it, so by switching the current on and off you can switch the magnetism 'on' and 'off' too. What's more, you can reverse the poles of the magnet by reversing the flow of the current. So you can use electromagnets to attract, repel, lift, pull or push other magnets at will. Maglev trains use powerful electromagnets built using superconducting materials. These create a stronger magnetic field, but are much lighter than normal electromagnets – which is ideal if you're trying to lift hundreds of tonnes of train carriage (and the passengers inside) and shift them along at high speed.

But how do they make the train move?

That depends on the Maglev system. Some use permanent magnets in the track, and stick the electromagnets under the train. Others do the opposite – putting permanent magnets under the train, and the electromagnets in the track. But in both cases the electromagnets are controlled by a computer system that switches them on and off in sequence, creating a ripple of magnetic fields along their length. These alternating magnets both pull the train (using magnetic attraction) and push the train (using repulsion) at once. This speeds up the train. To slow down, they simply do the opposite. If you were on the train, you wouldn't notice any of this, of course. It all happens so smoothly and silently that you hardly feel it accelerating at all. And before you know it you're whipping along at up to 300mph.*

Brilliant! So where can I ride one?

Right now, the only ones in regular use are in China and Japan. The Shanghai Airport Transrapid Maglev has been running since 2002, whipping passengers over the 19-mile stretch between the airport and city in a little over seven minutes. Japan Railways currently owns the world's fastest Maglev train, which runs on a 27-mile test line in Yamanashi prefecture, near the famous Mount Fuji. They're also planning to build a permanent Maglev line between Tokyo and Osaka, which will cover the 300-mile distance in about one hour. Europe and the US don't yet

* To find out how fast they can really go, and learn about the world's other speediest things, see *What's the fastest thing on Earth?* (page 247).

have any permanent Maglev lines, but many may be built over the next ten years. The planned SwissMetro line will link Geneva in Switzerland with Lyons in France, using an underground Maglev train that floats inside a 62-mile tunnel. And in the US, plans are underway for a Maglev line between Anaheim, California, and Las Vegas, Nevada. That one should hit an average speed of about 310mph.

So, with all these floating trains in the works, floating buses can't be too far behind, right?

Unfortunately we might have to wait a bit longer for those.

Why's that?

Because, unlike trains, buses run on roads instead of rails. They need to be free to make turns, change routes and take different paths from A to B. So floating Maglev buses would need magnetic roads and a complex control system to keep them running safely. Even if this was possible – which at the moment it's not – it would be extremely expensive, and no town or city could afford to build them.

Gah. No floating cars either, then?

Afraid not. Not using the Maglev system, anyway. That said, a few flying 'hovercars' using aircraft-type jet or turbofan engines have already been built, so they might come into use first. And some organizations (including NASA) are even attempting to build anti-gravity machines that could levitate a vehicle by 'cancelling out' the force of gravity, rather than fighting it with magnetism.

Anti-gravity? Could that work?!

Well, there haven't been any successes yet, and many physicists say it'll never work. A few, though, are still optimistic that it will.

Wow! That'd be excellent, wouldn't it? Will you tell me if they do it?

Sure. No problem. I'll float by your house in my new hovercar and let you know.

Practical science: five as-yet-unbuilt floating propulsion devices that Glenn would like to see

Jaglev – like Maglev, but it looks like a posh, expensive car

Baglev – enables your bag to levitate, so you don't have to carry it

Naglev – a floating mechanical horse

Haglev – in which you sit behind an ugly witch on a floating broomstick

Leglev – a pair of Maglev shoes that lets you float instead of walk

---

Brain Teasers

For all the things we know about the human body, we still have lots left to learn about the human brain. Our brains let us think, learn, remember, imagine, invent and more. They've allowed us to reshape our environment, to build societies and civilizations, and to dominate every other species on the planet.

But so much about the brain remains a mystery to us. How does it make memories? How do brains lead to minds and personalities? And why – one guy wants to know – are brains so ugly?

Here we explore the weird world of the brain, and have a crack at these and more questions along the way.

Some questions, however, won't be answered here. Such as:

You got a question from:
Name: Jessica
Question: Why are people so mean?

You got a question from:
Name: Pizky
Question: Why are my parents (especially my dad) so weird???

Some things, you just have to find out for yourself . . .

What makes human brains cleverer than animal brains?

In short, billions more brain cells and one massive section of forebrain. Other than that, human and other animal brains are more or less the same.

More or less the same?! How can a human brain be almost the same as a monkey brain? Or a mouse brain, even? We're *waaaay* cleverer than they are. Our brains must be completely different . . .

Well, they are different, but not as different as you might expect. For starters, monkey, mouse and human brains are all made of the same stuff – largely nerve cells (or *neurons*), clustered and linked together to form complex networks. They all contain millions of glial cells – which support and insulate the neurons. They all share similar regions – such as the spinal cord and brainstem, which receive inputs from sensory nerves in the muscles, organs and skin. They all have regions within the brainstem that control automatic body functions like breathing* and blood pressure. They all have regions at the base of the brain (where it joins on to the brainstem) that help in learning how to walk, run and jump. And they all have a region called the cerebrum that helps in learning, remembering and figuring things out.

But in human brains some of these regions have become enlarged, making us cleverer in certain ways.

---

* For more about how the brain controls breathing, see *Could we ever forget to breathe?* (page 175).

So, basically, we're smarter than other animals because we have *more* brain than they do?

Partly, yes. Large animals like humans and elephants will, of course, have bigger brains than tiny animals like mice. But even for large-bodied animals, humans still have freakishly huge brains.

The average adult human weighs about 70kg and carries a 1.5kg brain around. So the brain is about 2.1% of the total body weight. The brain of a full-grown Asian elephant weighs about five times as much as ours – 7.5kg. But that's only about 0.15% of its five-*tonne* body weight. So total brain size has a little to do with it, but it's not the whole story.

Is it how big our brains are compared to our body size?

That isn't quite it either. A mouse's brain weighs about 3.3% of its total body weight, so compared to their body size, their brains are much bigger than ours! And mice are clearly no more intelligent than us. So it's not just that *our brains are enlarged*, it's *which bits of our brain are enlarged* that makes us humans as clever as we are.

So which bits are they?

The bits contained within the cerebrum – otherwise known as the telencephalon. 'Telencephalon' means 'outer head', and describes the big, cauliflower-like bulbs that form a kind of wrinkly rind around the rest of the brain.* This is where we're so different to other animals. In humans, the rest of the brain has grown in proportion

---

* To learn more about why the brain is shaped this way, see *Why do brains look like ugly cauliflowers?* (page 171).

to our bodies. But the telencephalon has swelled to a huge size, giving us most of the abilities that mark us out from other animals.

What's so special about that bit, then?

It contains millions of densely packed neurons, which are linked together in more complex ways than those in any other region of the brain. It's these cells that give us our amazing ability to understand the world around us and to learn and remember complex skills. These are the abilities we're really referring to when we talk about 'cleverness'. This is also why we're so impressed by animals that can learn or remember new tricks, over animals that are 'clever' in other ways.

What do you mean by that?

Well, plenty of animals are 'clever' or 'smart' in any number of ways that don't necessarily involve learning new things. Some birds can weave themselves nests like baskets, which are much like human works of art. Termites

build immense mounds, which to them are the size of skyscrapers, without the aid of architects or construction machines. Some whales can navigate vast oceans reading the Earth's magnetic field as if it were a map. Yet we don't often think of these animals as 'clever'. We usually reserve that label for animals, like chimpanzees, that show *human-like* skills such as using sticks as tools. Or for animals that we can *see* learning new skills during their lifetimes – such as parrots that talk, or dogs that follow, stay and roll over on command.

Oh. Never thought about it like that before.

What's more, we also seem to have sympathy for – or empathize with – animals with learned abilities like this. Which, if you think about it, is why many of us are happy to keep cats and dogs as clever pets, but few of us are happy about eating them. Likewise, eating 'stupid' turkeys and chickens is fine, but eating parrots is not. Eating fish is good, but eating dolphins is bad. And so on.

But don't we avoid eating dolphins and parrots because they're rarer than fish and chickens?

True. But some fish, like Atlantic cod, are rarer than some dolphins. Yet plenty of people are still happy to eat cod. So it seems that, for most people, it's OK to eat pretty much any animal – so long as it's not too clever. And the only difference between what we call a 'clever' animal and what we call a 'stupid' animal lies in one bit of expanded brain.

Weird. So are you saying we should stop eating stupid animals, or start eating clever ones?

Neither. I'm just saying that when it comes to thinking about animals, we shouldn't always let 'cleverness' decide how we view them. This is especially important for rare or endangered animals. Many of the world's most endangered animal species are frogs, newts, birds and insects – none of which we think of as clever, but that shouldn't make them any less valuable to us, and shouldn't stop us from wanting to protect them.* We humans should be happy that we are so clever, but should also try to appreciate all other animals – whether they're clever by our standards or not.

You mean we're big-brained, but we don't have to be big-headed?

Spot on. That's a 'clever' way of putting it!

---

* For more about endangered animals, see *Will global warming hurt animals?* (page 94).

Sci-facts: brain weights and body weights

We humans have large, heavy brains. Other large animals have large brains too – but, compared to the size of their bodies, their brains aren't as big and as bulky as ours. This has a little to do with how we got to be so clever. But *which parts* of our brains are bigger and better developed is also important. Which is why mice are smart, but aren't likely to beat us at chess any time soon.

Animal	Brain (kg)	Body (kg)	Brain compared to body
Mouse	0.0004	0.012	3.3%
Human	1.5	70	2.1%
Dog (small)	0.072	11	0.65%
Cat	0.03	5	0.6%
Chimpanzee	0.42	70	0.6%
Owl	0.002	0.4	0.5%
Dog (large)	0.150	40	0.38%
Dolphin	1.5	500	0.33%
Elephant	7.5	5,000	0.15%
Horse	0.53	500	0.11%
Cow	0.5	500	0.1%
Sperm whale	7.8	13,500	0.06%

Why do brains look like ugly cauliflowers?

The wrinkles on the brain's surface might not look too pretty, but they help speed up the brain by keeping nerve cells closer together and shortening the connections between them.

Is that why it's so ugly, then?

I don't think brains are *that* ugly . . .

Yes, they are. *Seriously* ugly. They're all grey and wrinkly and puffy and . . .

All right, all right. So they're not the best-looking things in the world. But they're built to do a job, not to look pretty. And, to be fair, most of your other internal organs aren't that pretty either. Your heart looks like a small, meaty, partially deflated football covered in pulsing veins and arteries. Your lungs look like two wet, spongy sacks. And your intestines look like giant, slimy worms. But since they're tucked away inside your body nobody gets to see them, anyway. Same thing goes for the brain. Don't you think?

Yeah, but at least the other organs are smooth and rounded — not all wrinkly and gross . . .

What's the big deal about wrinkles?

Ugh. Don't like 'em, that's all.

Well, without them, our brains wouldn't be able to do the incredible job they do.

Why not?

To understand that, we'll have to go back a bit, and look at how the brain evolved . . .

Like all other bits of the body, the brain evolved to do a job. While other animals rely on their teeth, claws, powerful bodies or clever camouflage to survive, our species has got to where it is largely by using its head. We use complex tools, tactics, memories and learning to survive and thrive. But we couldn't do this without evolving large, complex, powerful brains. And with that comes a problem.

What's that?

Big, complex brains take a lot of energy to build, maintain and use. In fact, even though your brain makes up just 2.1% of your whole body weight, it uses 15% of the blood and 20% of the oxygen in your body. And that's after it's been built. In toddlers, the growing brain uses up to 60% of the energy available to the whole body. Brains are big, energy-hungry organs. So although our brains grew bigger on our route from small mammal to brainy ape, they couldn't just *keep on* getting bigger forever. Not only would they use up too much energy, but they'd also be difficult to support and protect at the top of spindly necks and bodies. So the brain needed another way of becoming more powerful, besides just getting bigger. And that's where the wrinkles came in.

How did they help?

The wrinkles, or *sulci* as they're called by neuroscientists, are actually folds in the *cerebral cortex*, which is the outermost region of the brain. These folds helped get around the brain size problem by making it more compact and efficient.

How'd they do that?

Our animal ancestors' brains needed all the brain cells (or *neurons*) they had, and they couldn't really make these cells any smaller than they already were. So, instead, the folds increased their brain power by bringing a larger number of brain cells into close contact with each other. This clever 'brain origami' shortened the distance between groups of neurons in different parts of the cortex, *speeding up* the signals sent between them. It also allowed *more connections* to be made between more pairs of neurons, which made the brain's circuits more complex. All this allowed more advanced brain functions – like the ability to learn complex tasks – to develop.*

So do other animals have the brain wrinkles too?

Some, but not all of them. And that was one of the clues that scientists had as to how brains have evolved and developed using these folds or sulci. Human brains have them, as do the brains of some other intelligent mammals like monkeys, apes and dolphins – though their brains

---

* For more about the differences between human and (other) animal brains, see *What makes human brains cleverer than animal brains?* (page 165).

are less folded than ours. Cat, dog and mouse brains have folds too – though fewer still than those of monkeys, apes and dolphins. Bird, reptile and fish brains have no folds at all, and by the time you get down to jellyfish, there isn't even a solid brain to speak of – just a web or net of nerve cells. In some jellyfish, you can even see these while they're still alive, by looking straight through their transparent bodies.

Yuck. Glad you can't see through my head and see *my* brain. Gross.

Look – your brain is a beautiful, sophisticated bit of biology, right? It may even be the most complex structure in the entire Universe! You should respect it for that, at least.

Yeah, but it still *looks* gross. Like a big, meaty cauliflower bulb covered in wrinkly ...

I give up.

Could you ever forget to breathe?

Happily, no. As long as you're healthy, your breathing continues automatically throughout your life. An ancient 'autopilot' system in your brain controls your breathing so that you don't have to worry about it.

Duhhh. Of *course* you keep breathing while you're alive. I knew *that*. I meant, could you ever — you know — stop doing it? Like by accident or something?

As long as your airway (the route from your mouth or nose to your lungs) isn't blocked and your body remains healthy and undamaged, then no. Your brain will take care of it, never missing a breath.

But you can miss a breath if you want to, right? All you have to do is hold it.

That's true, you can.

And you can breathe faster or slower on purpose, just by thinking about it.

Right. Also true.

So how does your body know to start breathing again when you stop thinking about it? And couldn't the autopilot forget to kick in? Just once?

Not really, no. Because the truth is, as long as your brain remains healthy and undamaged, the 'autopilot' never really shuts off. You can override it temporarily by concentrating on changing your breathing, but it's always there, in the background. And, if you try to do anything it *really* doesn't want to do, it can override you right back.

How does that work?

It's mostly controlled by nerves that run through your spine and into the base of your brain. These spinal nerves are bundled together into one big, thick nerve cable called the spinal cord. Within this, sensory nerves carry information from all over the body to the brain, and motor nerves carry signals from the brain back to the body.

At the top of the spinal cord are three bits of the brain called the medulla, the pons and the cerebellum (or 'little brain'). These process signals from the spinal cord and send signals back to the organs and muscles of the body. Together, these regions control most of the functions of your body that happen 'automatically'.

The medulla controls fairly simple automatic actions (or reflex actions), such as coughing and vomiting, and also partly controls your breathing and blood pressure. To control breathing, it sends three types of signals to the muscles of the lungs. Basically, the first type means 'fill the lungs', the second means 'stop filling the lungs' and the third keeps the whole in-out rhythm regular.

So if this rhythm goes chugging on all the time, what happens when we eat or drink something? How does it know to stop breathing in when we swallow, so we don't drown or choke?

Good question. That's because the medulla gets information from sensory nerves in the throat, which are activated when the throat is filled out or stretched. So, when you swallow a lump of food or a gulp of water, the medulla adjusts the signal pattern – sending out the 'stop filling the lungs' signal for long enough for the food or water to be swallowed, leaving the airway clear again. And helpfully – since the medulla also controls the coughing and vomiting reflexes – it can still 'take care of business' even if it all goes wrong. If the food sticks in your throat or you accidentally inhale the water, then vomiting and coughing can help clear it out again.

So the medulla is that autopilot bit of your brain you were going on about?

Well, it's part of the autopilot system, but not all of it. The other two bits I mentioned before, the pons and cerebellum, also chip in to help fine-tune your breathing to what condition your body is in, or what you're up to from moment to moment. Together, the medulla, pons and cerebellum receive information from sensory nerves and receptors in your eyes, skin, blood and elsewhere in your brain. Putting all this information together, these three brain regions then adjust your breathing pattern in response to muscle activity, altitude, temperature, stress, sleep and even emotions. All in all, it's a very clever 'autopilot' system that does more than just keep your breathing chugging along – it adapts to your every need, and never lets you down.

All right, then — what if you really *tried* not to breathe? Like, on purpose? Would it stop then?

Not for very long. After a while, the urge to breathe is just too great, and you have to breathe again, whether you like it or not. Even if you were strong (or stupid) enough to fight the urge, you would most likely pass out through lack of oxygen, and normal breathing would kick in again while you were unconscious. But this really wouldn't be a very clever thing to do, since you could damage your lungs (or even brain) in the process.

Yikes! Won't be trying that, then.

No – please don't.

So how long can you hold your breath for?

That depends on how fit you are, and how much air your lungs can take in at once (or your *lung capacity*). Trained athletes have higher lung capacities, so can generally hold their breath for longer. Divers usually manage the long-est – free divers (who dive without scuba gear) can stay underwater for more than seven or eight minutes at a time.* So if you want to increase your lung power – get fit. Smoking, on the other hand, will decrease your lung capacity, so avoid that like the plague.

Gotcha. Well — I'm glad I'll never forget to breathe, anyway. That's one less thing to worry about!

Yup – thanks to our brains, we can all breathe easy.

---

* And some people have managed almost twice as long as that! See *Why do we breathe, and why do we need lungs to do it?* (page 15), for more details.

Practical science: things you can't forget to do, versus things you can easily forget to do

Things you can't forget to do

Breathe

Blink

Sneeze

Cough

Vomit

Digest food

Pump blood

Hit the ground (when falling)

Exist

Things you can easily forget to do

Eat your breakfast

Feed the dog

Do your homework

Tidy your bedroom

Clean out the gerbil cage/fish tank

Pick up your house keys

Brush your teeth

Change your underpants

Wash

Do all people see the same colours?

No! People often see and interpret colours differently. Which is not surprising, since in a way colours don't really exist!

Eh? What do you mean, colours don't exist? Course they do. Grass is green, blood is red, poo is brown. Everybody knows that.

OK, fine. But why?

Why what?

Why is grass green? Why isn't it pink, or blue? Or no colour at all?

I dunno. It just is. You're supposed to be answering the questions here, not me . . .

All right, then – I'll tell you. It's green because we think it is.

What?! That doesn't make sense.

Yes it does. Perfect sense. Listen – grass is coloured because it contains a colour chemical, or *pigment*. As you may well know, beams of white light actually contain light of all colours of the rainbow – what physicists call the *spectrum* of visible light.

OK . . . with you so far . . .

Now each colour of light in the spectrum is actually just light at a slightly different frequency. Just like radio waves, which can be broadcast at different frequencies and picked up by radio sets tuned to receive them, light waves can have different frequencies too. Our eyes pick these up, and we interpret these different frequencies as different colours. We call the lowest frequency of visible light 'red'. The highest, we call 'violet'. And we call the frequencies in between 'orange', 'yellow', 'green', 'blue' and 'indigo'. All other shades – like pink, purple and brown – are names we give to mixtures of these six basic frequencies (or colours) of visible light.

O-kay. Got that. I think. So where do the pigment things come in?

What pigments do is reflect some frequencies of light, but absorb others. Grass contains a pigment called chlorophyll. This reflects the frequency of light we call 'green', and absorbs light of other frequencies. So *grass* is green because it reflects green light – but *green light* is green because that's what we call light at *that* frequency.

But if we all agree on what 'green' is, then we all agree that grass is green, right?

Ahh – now there's the thing, you see. We *don't* all agree on what green looks like. For starters, not all of us are able to tell the difference between light at different frequencies, so not all of us can tell the difference between, say, red and green light.

You mean colour-blind people?

They're the most obvious ones, yes. But even among those of us who are not colour-blind, people differ quite a lot in their ability to tell different colours apart. When tested, even two people with 'normal' colour vision will often disagree as to whether something is pure red or a reddish orange, whether it's pure blue or bluish green, and so on.

Why's that, then?

Partly because people are born with different types of colour-detecting eye cells. Visible light that enters the eye strikes a wall of cells at the back of it. There, three types of cells, called cone cells, contain pigments that change shape when struck by light. These pick up and recognize the different frequencies we call colours. Red cone cells detect 'red' frequencies, blue cone cells detect 'blue' ones, and you can probably guess what green cone cells do. But as the pigments in these three types of cell are controlled by genes – and not everyone has the same pigment genes – some people's cone cells work better than others. Hence, you might swear blind that the T-shirt you're wearing is green, but someone with different pigment genes will – quite literally – see it differently.

What's more, this doesn't just go for colours – people may also disagree over sounds, smells, tastes and other sensations too.

Why? Are their ear, nose and tongue genes different too?

In some ways, yes. The number of special sensor-proteins that detect smells and tastes – called chemoreceptors – can vary enormously between two different people, making their noses and tongues more or less sensitive to specific odours and flavours. But it also has to do with how we 'read' these sensations in the brain.

What do you mean, 'read'?

Well, your brain can only receive input from your eyes, ears, tongue, nose and skin in one way – as a series of pulses through your nerves. Every bit of information about the outside world – a sight, a sound, a smell, a taste – is turned into a coded signal within your sensory organs, and relayed to a specific part of the brain by sensory nerves.

So loud noises arrive in the brain as electrical signals. But so do bright lights, strong smells and sour tastes. The only major difference seems to be which bit of the brain they arrive at. There, your brain 'reads', or decodes, the signal, and interprets it with the help of your past memories.

So in a way, your brain takes input from your senses and creates a kind of 'virtual reality' to describe the world around you. The smell of a rotten egg, the taste of chocolate, the colour green, and the sound of a screeching violin don't really exist. They're just labels your brain creates – for certain chemicals in your food, or for certain frequencies of light and sound – to help you make sense of the world around you.

Weird.

It gets even weirder. In some rare cases, the brain can 'wire itself wrong' during development, leaving people with a strange condition called *synaesthesia*. These people may experience smells and colours in a piece of music, or taste potatoes whenever they hear a certain word. Probably because the coded signals representing sounds arrive in the wrong regions of the brain, or in many regions at once.

Crazy! Could I have that?

Well, there's only one way to find out.

What's that?

Go and smell your favourite tune and tell me what colour it is.

Practical science: top 10 names for synaesthetic music groups

1 Smells Like Purple
2 Spicy Sounds
3 Egg Flat Minor
4 The Tasty Blues
5 Cauliflower Sunrise
6 The FishTones
7 Bread Zeppelin
8 Tuba-stank
9 (Cheese) Curls Aloud
10 The Meatles

Which bit of your brain does your mind live in?

In all of it – and maybe even in other parts of the body too. Your brain is just a collection of nerve cells, but your mind is the result of how they interact.

Come on — your mind must live *somewhere*. It can't just be all over.

Why do you say that?

Well, different bits of the brain control different things, don't they? Like one bit controls your left leg, and another one your right. One bit does hearing, and another one does sight. Right?

Yup – that's partly true. Different parts of your brain's *motor cortex* control muscles in different parts of your body. Bits of the *somatosensory cortex* detect touch and temperature on different areas of your skin. And there are *visual, auditory* and *olfactory* areas that detect and process sights, sounds and smells.

So there must be a bit for memories, and another bit you *think* with.

Well, that would be neat and tidy, but it's not as simple as that. Even the motor and sensory areas interact with other parts of the brain to coordinate muscle movements and interpret the things you see and hear. Whenever you walk, run or ride a bike, cells in the motor cortex have to signal back and forth with cells in the cerebellum and other regions to 'remember' how to do it and coordinate the whole movement. Whenever you watch a passing car, your brain's vision centres interact with other regions to interpret the shape you're seeing as 'a car', to track its movement and to recognize other features (such as what colour it is, and what make of car it might be). So even fairly simple actions like these involve several different regions of the brain. As for memories, thoughts and feelings, brain scans and experiments have shown us that these involve using many areas – right throughout the brain – all at once.

So the thinking and memory areas are scattered about, then?

Actually, it goes a bit deeper than that. While some parts of the brain's outer layer (or *cerebral cortex*) are used more during complex thought than others, these regions still need to interact with lots of others for thoughts and memories to form. That said, brain cells (or neurons) in different parts of the brain don't really differ that much. The neurons of the 'vision' region look much like those in the 'hearing' region. The neurons that control your right big toe look much like those that control your left eyelid. And the neurons in the outer brain look just like those in the inner regions. The only real difference is the number and type of connections between them, and how they're primed to fire off signals.

But, if different bits of the brain look the same, how can it do so many different and complicated things?

It seems that the most complex functions of the brain – like remembering, learning and thinking – happen through web-like interactions between brain cells, rather than just within the cells themselves. Each individual cell might be simple, and they all might look similar. But each cell can trigger (or prevent) signals being fired from hundreds or thousands of others. The sum of these interactions – maybe millions at a time – produces the patterns and codes that we call thoughts or memories. Quick thoughts and short-term memories stick around as long as the same cells keep triggering each other, using a looping pattern of signals. Longer-term memories and learning probably happen as the cells remodel themselves into permanent networks, so that the same signalling pattern can be created easily, again and again. In this way, complex functions – like thoughts and memories – emerge from cells that *seem* too simple to perform them.*

So it doesn't really matter what kind of cells they are, or where they are in the brain?

A little, but not so much. What really matters are the connections between them. Your *brain* is just a bunch of brain cells. But your *mind* – what you think, what you learn, what you remember and what makes you ... well ... *you* – emerges from how those cells interact.

---

* For more about how the brain creates memories, see *Why does music bring back memories?* (page 190).

Whoa. That's pretty deep.

It gets better. If you think of feelings or emotions as part of your mind too, then your mind stretches beyond your brain. Outside your head, even.

What? How?

Other regions of your body contain neurons too. The spinal cord – which runs down the length of your back-bone – contains about a billion of them. While these are mostly involved in 'automatic' actions or reflexes in your body, they can also be affected by mood-altering brain chemicals like serotonin. This may be why you feel 'shivers' down your spine by just thinking about something scary. So, if your spine is involved in that thought or emotion, then doesn't that make it part of your mind too?

Now this is getting too weird . . .

Your intestines (or guts) have millions of neurons too – almost as many neurons as your spinal cord does – and over 90% of the serotonin in your body sits within these gut neurons. That might explain why many cultures think of emotions as *beginning* in the gut, rather than the brain. (When Japanese people get angry, they say their 'guts are standing up'!) We often talk about having 'gut instincts', or 'knowing it in my gut'. We all know the feeling of having 'butterflies in our stomachs' when we're nervous. And when you feel fear, love or nervousness 'in your gut', it's your gut neurons interacting with those in your brain that causes it. It's almost like having a second brain down there – or an assistant brain, at the very least.

I could do with an assistant brain, I think.

Why's that?

I think mine is full.

Nahh – plenty of room left in there, I'm sure. Just keep on reading – we'll get there!

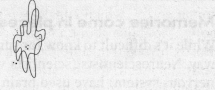

Why does music bring back memories?

We still don't know much about how memories are formed, but one idea is that the brain stores memories in pieces, rather than whole. So a piece of music might be the one especially strong piece of a memory that leads you to the rest of it.

Memories come in pieces?

While it's difficult to know for sure, it certainly seems that way. Neuroscientists (scientists who study the brain and nervous system) have used brain scans and clever experiments for many years to try and locate how and where memories form. From this work, it seems that a single memory may be *created* in just one part of the brain, but *stored* throughout a number of different sites. So somewhere along the line, the memory is broken into pieces. And whenever you recall a memory, you're actually bouncing nerve signals between all these pieces to recreate the whole. A bit like a 'join the dots' puzzle that reveals an entire picture once it's completed.

Why would your brain do that? Why not just store the whole thing all in one place?

It could help increase the amount of storage space available to your brain, by reusing similar bits of memories, instead of creating each new one from scratch. And it might also help organize your memories so that you can make sense of them. The memory of what an apple is, for example, could be split and linked to others, such as those of fire engines, tennis balls and bananas. So when you think of 'apple', you create an idea of it by comparing it to other 'red things', 'small, ball-shaped things' and 'fruit'. That way, you don't have to store every possible bit of information about every new thing you encounter. You only have to store what makes it *different* from other, similar things. This makes the amount of information in each memory smaller, and saves on overall memory space. Get it?

I think so. But how exactly are memories made? I mean, what do they *look* like?

Neuroscientists are pretty certain that short-term (or temporary) memories are created by linking groups of neurons (or brain cells) into circuits or loops. Neurons look a bit like tiny octopuses with thousands of tentacles. One cell might connect to thousands of others by growing a tentacle towards each one. There are billions of neurons in your brain, making trillions of connections with each other, so the whole thing forms a vast, complex web of tentacle contacts. But nerve signals don't flow equally well down every tentacle. Some tentacles allow signals to pass freely between cells, others block signals and others are somewhere in between. So, when you form a new memory, your brain creates a unique shape for it, by reinforcing the flow of signals between one particular group of neurons, through one big loop or circuit of tentacles.

OK . . .

But this change is only temporary, and in order to store the memory for any longer than a few hours, you have to turn it into a long-term memory. Neuroscientists know much less about how this works, but many think it happens by growing new, permanent tentacle linkages between cells. So, as you learn and remember new things, your brain is constantly reshaping and remodelling itself, building new circuits and loops that nerve signals can flow through. All you have to do is trigger one part of a memory – say, by hearing a piece of music, and the signal will flow through the rest of the circuit almost automatically, bringing back other details of that music and what you associate with it. That's one idea of how it might work – but it's very hard to know for sure what really happens with long-term memories.

Why's that?

Because while it's fairly easy to study someone forming a temporary (or short-term) memory, studying long-term memories means testing and observing the same people for years, or even decades. And it's difficult to compare old memories with the events that originally caused them – since the events may have happened so long ago that there's no accurate description of what *really did* happen.

So whereabouts in your brain are the memories kept? Are the old ones kept in the back, like the dodgy clothes in the back of your wardrobe?

Well, again it's hard to say, since long-term memo-ries are so difficult to study. But they all seem to begin life as short-term memories. And we're fairly sure *they* form in a region at the front of your brain called the pre-frontal cortex, or PFC. From there, they either disappear (if the memory is forgotten), or are transferred elsewhere in the brain, and turned into permanent, long-term memories there.

How do we know they form at the front of your brain?

Because people who suffer brain damage to that area can't form any new memories. They can be fine in every other way, but lose the ability to remember anything new.

Weird.

Also, the PFC region is much bigger in the brains of primates (like humans, apes, monkeys and lemurs) than in those of other animals. So that could explain why we (and the other primates) show a better ability to *learn* than most other animals.* Basically, we're better at learning stuff because we're better at remembering stuff.

Is learning the same as remembering, then?

No, but you can't have the first thing without the second. Think about it. Let's say you learned something new, like how to do your times tables in maths, then forgot it completely a week later. Did you really *learn* your times tables, or did you just remember them for a while?

Oh yeah. I see what you mean, now.

If short-term memories aren't made permanent, they're lost, and you can't really learn from them. So you can't really learn without forming long-term memories. This

---

* For more about the differences between human and (other) animal brains, see *What makes human brains cleverer than animal brains?* (page 165).

also partly explains why elderly people tend to be both more forgetful and less able to learn than young people. As you age, your brain becomes more rigid and less able to form new connections. So it's harder for old people to remember or learn new things. (People often say 'you can't teach an old dog new tricks', and this might explain why.) On the flipside, children's brains are so 'soft' and easily moulded that new connections are forming all the time. This could lead to extra links or 'short circuits' forming between unrelated memories. This might explain why kids often 'remember things wrong', and maybe also why they seem to experience déjà vu more often than adults.*

Yeah, and why is it that I can remember some things but not others?

Like what kinds of things?

Like, I can remember all the words to my favourite songs. But I can't remember friends' phone numbers without looking them up. Or famous people and dates in history, at school.

Well, like I said, there are still a lot of things we don't know. But one thing psychologists and neuroscientists have noticed is that people tend to create memories and learn more easily if they involve images, sounds (and even smells and textures) rather than words or numbers alone.

So pictures and music help make stronger memories?

Something like that, yes. Which might be why music can

---

* For more about this, see *What's déjà vu, and why do some people get it more than others?* (page 215).

trigger a memory you haven't thought of in ages – the music was the strongest part of it, and recalling it activates the rest of the memory 'circuit' we talked about earlier. But you can also use this effect in reverse, on purpose, to memorize things that are otherwise tricky to remember.

How's that?

It could be that you can't remember those names, dates or numbers you were talking about because they're too 'ordinary' or too 'uninteresting' to your brain. Some people get around this by using special memory techniques, like linking a word to an image, or a number to a sound. So, when you want to, you can 'smell' the answer to 12 x 12, or 'see' the image that reminds you of a person's name.

Huh? Don't get it.

Let's say you wanted to remember the names of two British Prime Ministers. For Tony Blair, you might imagine him as Tony Hair (as it rhymes well enough) – and see a picture in your mind of a man in a suit, standing outside 10 Downing Street covered with so much hair that it's growing out of his shirt and cuffs, and you can't see his face. For Gordon Brown . . .

. . . a big lump of stinky brown poo outside 10 Downing Street?

Err . . . if you like. That's the idea, anyway. So when you get a question about 'Prime Ministers' in a test or exam question, just seeing the words makes you think of the silly image of Tony Hair, with the long, flowing locks.

. . . or smell the poo outside Downing Street for Gordon Brown?

Err . . . right. Whatever works best for you. And the best thing is, the more you do this, the better your memory recall gets. It's a bit like 'memory exercise' for your brain.

Brilliant! I'm gonna memorize every book in my bag, ace all the tests at school and then — hang on —

What's up?

I can't remember where I put it.

What, your book?

No, my bag.

Better start exercising that brain . . .

Why do we need sleep?

Sleep could be a way of putting the brain into a kind of 'standby' mode while it learns, builds memories and remodels itself. In any case, we can't stay healthy for long without it.

Weird. Why would your brain need a 'standby' mode? Is it trying to save power?

Not really. Or at least if it is, sleep doesn't seem to be a very good way of going about it.

What do you mean?

Well, it's true that during sleep, your body generally uses a lot less energy than it does while you're awake. Which makes sense, if you think about it. When you sleep, you're lying down, so the muscles in your legs, spine and neck don't have to work at keeping you upright. You're also hardly moving, so the other muscles can stay relaxed too. And your eyes are closed, so your brain saves on the huge amount of energy it uses during waking hours to process the constant barrage of images taken in by your eyes – thousands per minute, all day long. But even while your body is at rest, your brain is still active during sleep. Very active, in fact.

So what is it doing?

Neuroscientists (scientists who study the brain and nervous system) are still working on the answer to that question. But they've learned a lot already by scanning the brains of healthy volunteers while they sleep, and many think that sleep might be linked to learning and forming memories.

But why would we need sleep to do that? Aren't we learning and remembering things all the time?

Yes, we are – but it doesn't happen by magic. Our brains process the things we see, hear, smell, taste, feel and do, and use these experiences to create memories. How long these memories last varies from less than a second to an entire lifetime. Some memories lead to learning; others don't. It depends how long they stick around for – as both memories and learning can both be lost or forgotten over time.

Why's that, then?

How it all works is still not clear, but it seems that long-lived memories and learning are stored differently in the brain to short-lived (and easily lost) memories.* Short-term memories are formed by small, temporary changes in the way nerve cells interact with each other. But when long-term memories are formed, the brain actually remodels itself – growing and building new connections between nerve cells, and permanently changing the shapes and structures in many parts of the brain. It's like a computer rearranging its own circuits to upgrade itself.

Wow! That sounds pretty drastic . . .

Right. And you might not want to mess with the hardware while it's in the middle of an upgrade. So that could be where sleep comes in. Just like the way we put computers into a 'safe' mode while installing new parts or software upgrades, sleep might prevent problems during the 'memory upgrade' at the end of each day, by powering down our non-essential functions and senses for while.

---

* For more about how the brain creates memories, see *Why does music bring back memories?* (page 190).

In any case, it must be pretty important for brain function, as most animals with well-developed brains seem to do it. If you think about it, going to sleep is pretty risky in the wild. A sleeping animal (or person) makes an ideal late-night snack for a lazy predator. To get around this, some animals sleep by shutting down half their brains at a time so they can stay alert. But our human brains seem to need a deeper, more complete resting state for sleep to be of any use – perhaps because we learn and remember more, and in more complex ways, than any other animal.*

So what happens if you decide not to sleep at all?

Sooner or later it usually catches up with you, and your brain lulls you into sleep whether you like it or not. But some people have sleep disorders such as insomnia, which prevent them from sleeping for days (or rather nights) on end. These people (and others kept awake for long periods during experiments) usually suffer from the effects of sleep deprivation, including headaches, memory loss, confusion and learning difficulties.

---

* For more about the differences between human and (other) animal brains, see *What makes human brains cleverer than animal brains?* (page 165).

So how much sleep do we need?

That can depend on your own body type, your age and how active you are during the day. Most adults seem to need at least six hours to function properly, while children and teenagers may need more – eight hours minimum. That kind of makes sense, if you think about it – as school demands a lot of learning and memory formation. Some people – such as famous artist, inventor and all-round genius Leonardo Da Vinci – have tried to cram more hours into the day by sleeping in bursts or power-naps (Leonardo slept for thirty minutes out of every four hours, day and night, for a total of three hours of sleep per day.) But there's no evidence that this works any better than one good chunk of sleep. Plus it's kind of inconvenient, having to nap every few hours like a baby . . .

Not for me. I love sleep, me. I'd sleep all day if I could.

Well, it turns out that too much sleep isn't very good for you either. Sleep researchers have discovered that people who sleep too much (or for too long at once) can suffer from confusion and learning difficulties too. Plus it isn't very good for the rest of your body since muscles waste away and fat builds up as your metabolism slows down.

So what's the perfect amount of sleep?

For adults, probably about six to eight hours. For children, between eight and ten. So if you get up for school at 7 a.m. you really need to be asleep (not just in bed) some time between 9 p.m. and 11 p.m. Stay up until midnight, and you'll learn less the next day.

What if I went to bed at midnight, but got up for school at around 10 a.m. instead? That'd be the same amount of sleep, right?

Well, in theory ... yes ... but I'm not sure how happy your parents or teachers would be with you rolling into class an hour or two late every day.

But if everybody did it, then the whole school would get a lie-in!

True, but you'd also have to stay at school for a few hours later every day to make up for lost learning time ...

No way! That'd be like detention every day! Hmmm. Maybe I need to think this over a bit more . . .

You do that. I'm off to upgrade my snoozeware. Zzzzzzz.

Practical science: the power of sleep

Not getting enough sleep? Well, you should – cos you might be holding yourself back. Here are a few things you could get better at with eight to ten hours of sleep per night:

Maths, science, geography, languages – with your better memory and concentration, you'll be better able to figure things out and to learn new facts, words and methods.

Art, music, dance – getting enough sleep helps with creativity and with learning new motor (or physical) skills.

Sports and games – in addition to better motor skills, your reflexes will improve as you become more alert. Plus sleep helps the body to recover more quickly from injuries.

Flying – all right, sleep won't actually help you fly, but you might dream about it more often, and get good enough at it to fight crime or save the world in your sleep. Works for me.

Could we learn to read thoughts and move things with our minds?

There's no evidence yet that we could ever do this with our brains alone. But some people can communicate with and control machines using their thoughts – with the aid of implanted brain chips.

So you reckon mind-reading and psychic stuff is impossible, then?

I didn't say that. It's just that many people have claimed to be telepaths (mind-readers) and telekinetics (people who can move things with their minds alone), but so far there's been no proof – or even any decent evidence – that they can really do the things they say they can.

What about all those psychics and mind-readers you see on TV?

Most of them are pretty easy to explain. They use clever tricks and techniques to make it look like they have superpowers or psychic powers, when they clearly don't. Mind readers and psychics often learn sneaky mental suggestion techniques, using specific words, phrases or hand signals that cause people to think of certain words or images. Then they pretend to 'read' the person's mind and tell them what they're thinking of – when, really, they planted the thought there in the first place.

Yeah, right — that'd never work.

Really? OK. Then think of an object – any object. Maybe something from when you were younger . . . something you *really* wanted for Christmas . . . something you were really pumped up about getting . . . you spoke about it all the time, that thing you'd really *like* . . . turn the image around and around in your head . . . OK.

OK . . .

Chances are you were picturing a bike, right?

What?! How'd you know that?

Because I *put it* there, using key words and suggestions. If it didn't work – no big deal. But if it did – go back through the instructions and you'll see how I did it: object . . . from when you were younger . . . *really* (wheelie) . . . *pumped up* (tyres) . . . *spoke* . . . *like* (rhymes with bike) . . . *around and around* (go the wheels) . . . and so on. That was just a crude version of what trained magicians and 'mentalists' can do. It's called Neuro-Linguistic Programming (or NLP) because you use language (or linguistics) to 'program' someone's neurons (or brain cells) to create an image or memory.*

Do they all work like that?

Not all of them. Some performers instead use close observations about the 'victim's' clothes, appearance, speech, mouth and eye movements to tell what kinds of things they might be thinking of. Then they use specific questions to narrow it down before guessing, or use NLP to suggest something slightly different. Put it all together, and you get a pretty convincing telepathic act. But an act is all it is – they're not really communicating with another person, mind-to-mind. Same goes for mind-moving

---

* For more about the differences between human and (other) animal brains, see *What makes human brains cleverer than animal brains?* (page 165).

telekinetics. Many claim they can shift glasses, bend spoons, and more – but in reality it's usually a thin wire that's doing the moving, or it's a 'trick object' that's been specially treated to move or bend with small temperature or pressure changes.

All right, so maybe no one's done these things yet. But that doesn't mean no one *ever will*, right?

That's true, we can't know that for sure. But while there's no evidence at all that telepathy or telekinesis actually exist, most scientists aren't looking too hard for proof that they do.

Couldn't our brains evolve so that we might be able to do these things one day?

It's possible, but it doesn't seem very likely, for two main reasons. Firstly, it's not clear how the brain might evolve to do this. Some parapsychologists (people who use science-like methods to study unexplained 'spooky' phenomena like mind-reading and psychic powers) point out that the brain creates a magnetic field, and if we could learn to control or boost this, we might be able to signal

to other brains with it. Or even use it to move metallic objects – like an electromagnet.

Would that work?

It doesn't seem so, since the field is way too weak to move even the lightest object, or send even the weakest signal.

Boo. So what's the second reason?

The human brain has pretty much stopped evolving. And unless there was some huge advantage to being a mind-reader or telekinetic, then there would be no real reason for it to do so.

But being able to move stuff and chat to people with your brain would be brilliant!

Right – it would. But we can happily survive by moving stuff with our arms and legs, and chatting using our voices, tongues and ears. So there's nothing forcing us to evolve these extra abilities. But while we might not develop these skills naturally, some people think we might be able to do it using technology. In fact, there are already a few people out there who can communicate and move things with their minds.

There are? But you said —

I said no one could do it *with their minds alone*. But with a little help from a microchip implanted in the brain, one or two test subjects have used their thoughts to change TV channels, move computer cursors and even send emails.

Really?!

Really. Once implanted, these chips can detect electrical signals in the brain, translate them into commands and transmit them to computers and other devices. They're being developed for people who have been paralysed by accidents or disease, so that they can communicate and use machines even without the use of their voices and limbs. In the future, though, similar chips could be implanted even in healthy people, allowing them to operate doors and lighting or write letters and emails using their thoughts. We may even be able to communicate chip-to-chip, brain-to-brain, with a kind of computerized telepathy. Experts have nicknamed this 'techlepathy'.

That'd be superb! Like a mind-reading, superhero cyborg or something!

You'd have to totally master it though, if you wanted to keep any friends.

Why's that?

Well, you don't want to say *everything* you think out loud, do you?

Whoa! Good point.

Practical science: ten things not to think when chatting telepathically

1 Wow – that zit is huge . . .

2 Yeuch. If my dog's breath was that bad, I'd force-feed it Tic-Tacs.

3 Actually, I hate that band. I only pretend to like them because you do.

4 Bored, bored, borrrrrrrred.

5 I must change my computer password. '1234' is just too easy to crack.

6 Debbie was right – you are annoying.

7 . . . and your new haircut looks stupid.

8 If I keep quiet, she'll never know it was me. I mean, anyone here could have farted . . .

9 Did I put clean underpants on this morning?

10 . . . or this week?

What's the difference between a computer and a brain?

Brains are built very differently, have a different purpose and handle information in a different way, making them – for now at least – far more versatile and powerful than computers.

That can't be right. Computers think much faster than we do, don't they?

Actually, no they don't. In fact, computers don't think at all.

But aren't computers just like electronic brains? And brains like fleshy computers?

In some ways, yes. But in other ways – most ways, in fact – brains and computers are very different things.

Different, how?

For starters, they're built and structured very differently – and it turns out that how they're built has a huge effect on how they work, and limits what they can actually *do*.

How's a computer built, then?

Well, that's quite a long story – but, if you stick with me, I'll give it a go. Here goes ...

When you look at a computer, you see a screen, a keyboard and a mouse. But these are just the input and output devices. Inside, all computers are built from electronic circuits. These are arranged and connected in complicated branching patterns, and contain thousands of little electronic gates or switches. The combined pattern of open and closed gates (or on/off switches) allows the computer to process and store information using a simple logic code. The earliest computers were mechanical and could only process numbers – like extremely posh calculators. Later computers had electronic switches controlled by valves, resulting in room-sized computers that could do more complex sums. But they couldn't handle more than one task at once, and took all day (and an enormous amount of power) to do even that.

Later still, the valves were replaced with a different type of electronic switch called a transistor. These were much smaller, faster and more reliable, and allowed a new generation of computers to handle different types of information, handle more than one task at once and be programmed to perform a wide range of functions. Soon, hundreds of these transistor switches were being printed on to tiny, flat circuit boards. Then engineers found a way of printing thousands of them on to a single, tiny silicon microchip. (By this time, computers were small enough to be placed on desktops and cheap enough to be bought by almost anyone.)

Finally, computer engineers started printing an entire computer's worth of circuits on to a single chip, called a microprocessor. That's what all modern desktops and laptops (not to mention mobile phones and other computerized gadgets) are based on.

Whoa. That was a long story.

Told ya.

So how's that different from a brain, then?

Like computers, brains have circuits, which are arranged in branching patterns and process information using

logic. But, rather than transistors, brains have nerve cells, or neurons. Neurons don't simply carry and switch electric currents, the way metal wires and circuits do. Instead, they carry signals through the ultra-fast movement of charged molecules (mostly sodium and potassium) and special signalling chemicals called neurotransmitters. These movements ripple from one end of the long, thin neuron to the other, like a fizzing bomb fuse.

In turn, this triggers the release of neurotransmitters at the end of the neuron, which might or might not trigger the next neuron to fire off its own signal. What's more, the junction (or synapse) between two neurons can be adjusted, so that it's either more or less likely to carry the signal between them. This means a neuron can do more than a simple electronic switch or gate, as in addition to 'open' or 'closed', it can be in a number of other states in between (a bit like being 'half open' or 'partially closed'). Because of this – and the fact that neuron 'circuits' are arranged in far more complex branching patterns that electronic ones – brains can handle far more information than computers, and they can process it far more quickly.

Hang on – no they can't. My computer can do sums way better than me. And it can store thousands of pictures and words, and never forgets a thing. I can't remember

anything like that many things, and I'm *always* forgetting stuff . . .

Well, it's true that computers are better than brains at raw number crunching. And the way they're built makes recalling words and images from memory easier for them than it is for us. But, believe it or not, your brain can handle way more information than even the most powerful computer – and it does it every day. For example – what happens to your computer if you try to open a really detailed picture, or download an entire movie? Does it open right away, or does it take a while?

It usually takes ages.

Right. And other programs – like Internet browser windows – often slow down while the computer tries to do it. This is because detailed images and video take up a massive amount of memory and processing power. Your computer can only use so much memory and power at once, and it has to split this between the images and the other programs in order to get the job done. Splitting the power means it takes longer to do each task.

Yet if you think about it, your brain is processing and storing continuous video images from your eyes every second, all day, every day. You don't remember every detail of what you see, because your brain is processing the images to weed out what's important. But they're still being processed. And often you're thinking about or doing other things (like riding a bike or talking) *at the same time* as you're processing all this. It might not seem like such a big deal to you, but to a computer, that amount of graphic data would be overwhelming. In fact, the maximum data processing rate (or *bandwidth*) of a brain isn't just way bigger than that of a computer – it's bigger than that of practically *every computer in the world* put together. So have some of *that*, Mister PC.

So brains and computers both have memories and process things, but brains just do it much better. And that's the big difference between them?

It's more than that, actually. They differ not only in how they work, but also in what they do. Basically, computers run programs, and process and store information. Brains can do all of this, but also learn complex tasks, control our bodies, control our behaviour and give rise to creativity and consciousness. While some computers have a limited ability to learn new skills (like playing chess or other games), none have been built yet with true creativity or consciousness. Nor do computers control their own behaviour. They may be able to self-diagnose problems and adapt to new information, but none of them actually 'think' in the way that we do. And that won't happen until real Artificial Intelligence (AI) is developed.

Don't we have any computers with that yet?

Not yet, but it's probably only a matter of time before we do. Which brings me to the final big difference between brains and computers ...

What's that?

How quickly they evolve. The human brain *is* way more powerful than even the most powerful computer. But then it had a 600-million-year head start. Modern electronic computers have only been around since the 1940s – when they were the big, clunky, room-sized monsters

I was telling you about. So they've come a long way in a very short time. Our brains are evolving little, if at all. But computers are evolving at an incredible speed. So it probably won't be too long before they start to catch up with us.

So what happens then?

Who knows. Maybe we'll be able to talk to them directly, using our voices instead of a mouse and keyboard. (Not just using single words and commands, but actually *talking* to them and *discussing* things with them.) We may even figure out how to share memories and thoughts, and make real computer friends. If they're friendly computers, that is . . .

What if they're not?

Well, you can always threaten to unplug them. Usually works for me when my computer plays up . . .

What's déjà vu, and why do some people get it more than others?

It could be a kind of 'misfire' in the brain, or it could simply be 'remembering things wrong'. The truth is, we don't yet know for sure.

A brain misfire?! Isn't that a bit dangerous?

Not at all. Brain cells are firing off all over the place, all the time. In fact, the only reason you can read this line is because nerve signals from your eyes are triggering thousands of nerve impulses in the brain region directly behind them. Even simple reading requires your brain to do many things at once. You have to sense the letters and words on the page, examine and recognize their shapes, and compare them with an immense list of pre-learned letters, words and phrases. Then you have to link them to ideas and concepts, and finally make sense of the whole sentence. All this happens in a matter of seconds, yet each step requires hundreds of nerves to fire, and triggers off the firing of hundreds more. If you could see inside your brain while you were reading, it'd look like a non-stop firework display.

Yikes! I never thought about it like that.

It sounds like a dangerous mess, I know. But for the most part, all this firing is incredibly well organized. The cells all fire off in precise sequences, and signals split, branch off and recombine in very precise ways to produce thoughts, memories and actions.

So whenever you get a misfire, you get déjà vu?

No – not really. 'Misfires' happen all the time, but because there are billions of nerve cells tracking out trillions of possible pathways through the brain, signals almost always make their way around misfires very easily. Déjà vu seems to involve just one specific type of misfiring, which only occurs during the formation of new memories. But as déjà vu doesn't seem to happen very often, this kind of misfire is probably quite uncommon. Of course, some people are more prone to déjà vu than others . . .

OK, but what have memories got to do with it?

Some scientists believe that memories are stored in pieces, rather than as a whole, and this might have something to do with déjà vu. Ordinarily, you take an experience (like something you've seen, heard or felt) and store it as a memory.* Later, when you see, hear or feel something similar, your brain recreates that memory and compares it with the new experience, allowing you to interpret things and learn from them. For example – you might hear a certain drum beat for the first time in the introduction to a song. Later, you hear a similar drum beat in another song. Ordinarily, your brain can recall the memory of the first song – but also recognize that it's different to the second – by comparing what you're hearing *now* to a recreated memory of what you heard *then*. Got it?

I think so . . .

OK. So déjà vu could happen when there's a subtle

---

* For more about how the brain creates memories, see *Why does music bring back memories?* (page 190).

misfiring during memory formation. This could cause the memory of the drum beat to form before you've registered it as a new experience – tricking you into thinking you *remember* it, when in fact you're just *experiencing* it. For most of us, this is a fairly rare and unique feeling. Of course, some people are more prone to déjà vu than others . . .

But why do . . .
Hang on a minute — you said that already.

No, I didn't.

Yes, you did. You said . . .
Oh, wait — I get it. Very funny.

Heh, heh. Sorry. Couldn't resist.

Whatever. But what about the
'remembering things wrong' bit?

Well, another explanation for déjà vu could be that some people who get it *think* they've seen or heard something before, when in fact they haven't. They may have seen something a bit similar – but not the same – and they're remembering the original thing, well . . . wrong.

Is that possible? I mean, you either
remember things or you don't, right?
At least, that's what I thought.

Actually, remembering things 'wrong' seems to be quite common. This is because we don't really 'recall' memories (like images and sounds) whole the same way a computer does. As we said earlier, memories seem to be stored in bits or pieces in several different parts of the brain. So when we 'remember' something, what we're probably doing is *recreating* the image, sound or feeling by piecing the bits back together again. Sometimes the whole is rebuilt perfectly. More often, there are bits missing, which is why you might be able to remember your fifth birthday but (unless you have a photograph) you might not remember what colour socks you were wearing. And sometimes the creative 'rebuilding' of a memory can weave in parts of other memories – or even of things you've never experienced yourself. In tests, scientists have discovered that most people do this at one time or another. So you might be *certain* you were wearing white socks on your fifth birthday . . . when you actually wore them to your seventh birthday party . . . and it was your best friend who wore the white ones at your fifth . . . while you were wearing white trainers and grey socks, and so on. It's easily done.

So some people might be trying to make an old memory fit a new thing?

Exactly. But we don't really know for sure, as déjà vu doesn't happen very regularly – so it's difficult to catch someone in the middle of a déjà vu experience and, say, brain scan them. And this makes it difficult for brain scientists to study. Of course, some people are more prone to déjà vu than others . . .

You said that already.

No, I didn't.

Yes, you did. You —
GAAAAGGGHH!! I fell for it *again*!!

Heh, heh.

Practical science: 'done it before' feelings, explained using cows

Déjà vu   feels like you've seen this cow before

Déjà moo   feels like you've heard this cow before

Déjà boo   feels like you've frightened this cow before

Déjà poo   feels like you've trodden in this cowpat before

Déjà ewww   yup, it was pretty gross last time too

The BIG Questions

Some questions are just so big that even science can't give us a definite answer. Try getting your head around this one, for example:

You got a question from:
Name: Ashley
Question: What will happen in 100,000 million years?

Beats me, Ashley. But I'll be happy if people are still around to find out.

We all love extreme things. The biggest, the smallest, the hottest and the toughest. Even if we never see them in our entire lives, just thinking about them can make the world around us seem less average and ordinary.

So here we celebrate the extraordinary. We'll meet the world's oldest animal, the world's deadliest disease, and find out what's wetter than water.

And to the writer of this question:

You got a question from:
Name: Camilla
Question: What is the size of the universe we really need to know this is an emergency thanksxx

Wow – that sounds serious. Perhaps you're defending the world from an alien invasion. Perhaps you're planning a trip to another Universe and you need to leave in a hurry.

Either way, I'm sorry I didn't get back to you, and I very much hope you managed to figure it out in time. Oh yeah, and good luck.

What are the smallest and biggest things alive?

Depending on how you measure them – and what you mean by 'alive' – the smallest thing is either a bacterium, a virus or a bit of mobile DNA. And the biggest is either a tree, a fungu, or the entire planet!

Boo. That's cheating. I mean, bacteria and viruses aren't really *alive*, are they? They're just kind of . . . well . . . *there*.

That depends how you look at it. Biologists will tell you that bacteria – at the very least – are *definitely* alive. And some might even go as far as saying viruses are alive too.

But I was thinking of a tiny mouse or a flea or something. You know — something that actually moves around. Eats things. *Lives*.

But bacteria *do* do all those things. Even though they don't have legs, many can contract tiny muscle-like rods and fibres inside their bodies to squidge around and look for food. Some even have little protein propellers called *flagella*, which drive them through liquids like a motorboat through water. And although they don't have mouths, they can certainly eat. Most absorb nutrients (which could be anything from sugars to metals), digest them using proteins called enzymes, and use them for energy or to build things inside their bodies. And, if you think about it, that's just what other living things do when they eat. Including us. We just eat and digest things in a more complicated way than bacteria do. Besides that – living things aren't identified by their ability to move around and eat things.

They're not? How do you know if something is alive or not, then?

Well, it's more to do with whether or not the thing *organizes* itself, and more importantly *reproduces* and *maintains* itself so that it (and its descendants) can go on 'living'. Bacteria definitely do this, since they absorb nutrients, copy their own DNA and reproduce by splitting in two, producing bacterial 'daughters' that will go on to do the same. Viruses copy their DNA, assemble themselves and reproduce too. And if you want to go even further, there are tiny strings of mobile DNA called transposons (or 'jumping genes') which insert themselves into a cell's DNA, copy themselves and 'jump' out again to insert themselves elsewhere. In a way, they're also organizing, reproducing and maintaining themselves.

So are *they* alive, then?

Well, sort of. But since viruses and transposons can't do all this alone (they have to hijack the copying machinery inside the living cells they invade), many biologists don't consider them to be 'alive' at all. A few say they are, and perhaps most say they contain elements of living and non-living things. So they're kind of on the edge or boundary of life as we know it. So the safe bet for the smallest things alive is bacteria, which are – in any case – *waaaay* smaller than mice or fleas.

Like *how* small?

The average mouse is about 12cm long, including the tail, and the average flea is about 3mm across. Bacteria come in a range of shapes and sizes, but a typical one (like *E. coli*, a bacterium that lives in your guts) is about 2 micrometres (two millionths of a metre, or two thousandths of a millimetre) across. To give you some idea of how small that is – you could lay about a thousand of them end to end across the head of a pin. Viruses and transposons are even smaller – 100–200 nanometres (or billionths of a metre) long. But we're disqualifying them here and crowning bacteria as the world's tiniest life forms. At least for now.

All right — so that's the small stuff sorted. What about the biggest things alive? Don't dinosaurs get a look in?

Well, some of them were pretty big, but you did say the biggest things *alive* . . .

Fine — whales, then. Aren't they bigger than trees and funguses?

Fungi.

Whatever.

That depends on the whale, the tree and the fungus. At over 34m long, the blue whale is the *largest animal* alive today. But, if we're talking about the *largest living things*, then some trees are way bigger than that. Giant sequoia trees grow up to 90m tall, up to 9m wide, and weigh more than *sixteen* blue whales. And that's just if you're looking at *individual* trees.

What do you mean by that?

Some trees, like quaking aspen trees, can clone themselves. They grow in clumps or stands that share the same roots. Since all the bodies or trunks in the clump are identical, you could say that they're all part of one big tree-body. If so, then one quaking aspen clump covers over 170,000 square metres and weighs nearly 6,000 tonnes – about the same weight as a giant sequoia tree, but much larger in volume.

And what's with the fungus?

Just like the aspen, some fungi clone themselves and grow to cover enormous areas of land. And since it's not clear where one fungal body ends and another begins, you could say that these are all one living thing too. One colony of honey mushroom, which grows in North America, has been found to weigh about 540 tonnes – or about one tenth as much as a giant sequoia. But the fungus covers almost 9 square kilometres of land, making it the biggest living thing in terms of how much space it takes up.

Is that the biggest, then?

Maybe. But one or two scientists have suggested that you could even think of the entire Earth – including its soil, atmosphere, oceans and all the things living in them – as one huge living thing or *superorganism*. If that's the case, then the largest living thing is about 12,800km wide and has a mass of about 5.5 billion trillion tonnes!

So the biggest living thing in the world is . . . the world?

You could see it that way, yes.

It must be pretty lonely, then.

Maybe not – there could be other living worlds out there in Space waiting for it. Perhaps we can help introduce them one day . . .

What's the oldest living animal, and how old does it get?

We can't be sure which animal lives longest, as the world's oldest animal may still be alive and undiscovered somewhere in the wild. But the oldest we've found is a kind of mussel that can live for over 405 years!

A mussel?! Like a little, squidgy, clam-type thing? I thought for sure it'd be a tortoise or a whale or something.

Well, they do live pretty long lives too. Giant Galapagos tortoises can live up to 177 years, and bowhead whales up to 211. In fact, many large animals live very long lives. According to zoo records, if they're healthy (and maybe a bit lucky), elephants and parrots can live up to seventy years, and swans for over a hundred years!

Why do they live so long?

No one knows for sure, but there are a few general patterns that give us clues. Size, for example, seems to be important. In general, the larger an animal is, the longer it lives. This helps to explain why giant whales and tortoises can live for over a century, while tiny mammals like shrews get less than three years, and tiny insects like mayflies less than a day.

But that clam-thing isn't very big, is it?

Good point. It isn't. In reality, there are plenty of exceptions to the 'bigger animals live longer' rule, so it's clearly not as simple as that. Another clue seems to suggest that it's not just *how big*, but *how active* an animal is that decides its lifespan. As larger animals are less active than smaller ones (think of a lumbering tortoise or whale versus a scurrying shrew), it may be that they live longer because they exert less effort just getting through life. Many small animals spend most of their time and energy scurrying around after food and away from predators – they're always 'on the go'. Large animals have fewer predators and, often, less mobile prey. Bowhead whales simply drift into underwater clouds of plankton for a meal, while giant tortoises pursue the not-very-fast-moving grasses and fruits of the Galapagos Islands. Similarly, the Icelandic cyprine – our 405-year-old mussel – just sits on a rock and filters its food out of the ocean. Not much effort needed there.

Getting old probably doesn't bother it much either. It doesn't have eyes or feet, so it doesn't need glasses or a walking stick when they wear out. And getting grey and wrinkly isn't a problem, since it basically started out that way, anyway.

And that's the oldest animal there is?

Well, technically there is one older. You might not think of sponges as animals, but they're classified as simple animals or *primitive metazoa*. If you count them, then there's

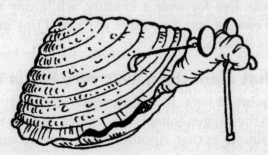

one kind – the glass sponge – which can live for an incredible 15,000 years! If you go beyond animals to other kinds of organism, some live even longer than that.

How much longer?

Some individual trees and plants can live for thousands of years – like bristlecone pines, which can live for maybe 5,000 years or more. Some other plants reproduce by budding bits of themselves off into new plants – in effect, cloning themselves. These cloned plants and trees cluster together, and while some parts of the cluster die off, the rest live on, and you could say the whole colony is one, big, living organism – like bits of the same plant body, rather than different individuals. If you count these, then the oldest plant found is a Tasmanian king's holly cluster found by Australian botanists in 1996. Using chemical dating methods, they found it was over 46,000 years old!

No way! Then that *has* to be the oldest living thing — right?

Well, again, that depends how you define 'living'. Some fungi and bacteria can turn into dormant (or practically lifeless) spores when their water or nutrient supply dries up, and then spring back to life millions of years later when watered and fed. Microbiologists have found spores of a *bacillus* (or 'rod-shaped') bacterium over 250 million years old, and successfully brought it back to life in the lab. Also, like plants, many fungi and bacteria simply bud off from each other to reproduce, growing in identical colonies or *clones*. Some of these, like some *archaean* (or 'ancient') bacteria, have been around for over *3.5 billion* years – since the beginning of life on Earth – and they're still going strong. In effect, they never age. They're immortal.

So if some things can live forever, why do other things get old at all?

Once again, no one can say for sure yet, but some scientists think it comes back to the idea of activity we were talking about earlier. Different organisms have different rates of metabolism – which is basically how fast they break down food and turn it into energy. Simple and small organisms tend to have faster metabolic rates, have to 'feed' constantly and often live at a high pace to sustain themselves. Larger, more complex organisms can often get away with eating a few times a day, have slower metabolic rates and are less active. It's thought that during daily life the process of breaking down food and turning it into energy might actually lead to ageing by damaging the DNA inside cells. So the more active the organism, the faster it 'burns out' and ages itself.

So the secret to living forever is to do as little as you can? Ha! I knew it! In that case, I'm just going to lounge around in front of the TV as much as possible from now on, and there's nothing my parents can do about it! Bwa ha ha haa!!

Unfortunately, that's not going to work, I'm afraid. In fact, that will probably do just the opposite. Our bodies and brains need exercise and stimulation to keep us looking, thinking and feeling young. Slobbing only leads to health problems as your body and brain weaken through too little use. From everything scientists know so far, staying fit seems to be the best way to stay younger for longer.

I guess it seems to work for that little clam-type thing, anyway.

Why do you say that?

Well, he obviously has mussel power.

Groan.

Heh, heh.

Why are massive cats called lions, tigers and leopards, but massive dogs are still called 'dogs'?

Because lions, tigers and leopards are different species from pet cats, whereas all pet dogs – from chihuahuas to Great Danes – are all the same species. Dog breeds only look so different because we've made them so – with a little help from doggie DNA...

All right, then — if they're all supposed to be the same animal, why do dog breeds look so different, when cats don't?

What do you mean?

I mean, you get different breeds of cat too, right?

Right. Short-haired, long-haired, skinny Siamese, fluffy Persians...

Yeah, but they're all more or less the same size and shape, aren't they? You don't get any massive pet cats the size of wolfhounds. Or super-fast racing cats like greyhounds. So why are dog breeds all so different?

Well, it's partly because we've made them that way on purpose. And it could be partly because dogs, as a species, were also quite easy to change.

How's that, then?

It goes something like this. Both dogs and cats started out as wild animals – our prehistoric ancestors only bothered to tame (or domesticate) them so that they could work for us. About ten thousand years ago, when humans started farming wheat and other cereals, cats came in handy to keep mice away from the grain. Much later, people adopted them as pets and started cross-breeding them to make them fluffier, cuddlier or more interesting to look at. But cats have basically only ever had two jobs: mouser or house pet.

What about dogs?

Dogs were domesticated thousands of years ago too – probably even earlier than cats. But, almost immediately, dogs came in handy for more than just one kind of job. Being natural pack animals, they not only joined and followed human 'packs' more enthusiastically than cats, but were also easily coaxed into guarding and hunting with their adopted human pack leaders. And whereas all domestic cats probably descend from those first tamed cats in the Middle East (where farming first began), dogs were probably tamed and adopted as hunters and guards in many different places – including Europe, Asia and Africa. As they were kept and bred separately, dogs on different continents developed slightly differently. Some were bigger, others were smaller. Some were skinny, others more chunky and muscular.

And that's how all the different shapes and sizes happened?

Not quite. That's where they started, perhaps, but these

early dog 'breeds' still looked pretty similar. It wasn't until the last few hundred years that breeders created most of the dog breeds (over 150 of them) we know today – by cross-breeding dogs with special characteristics to produce more breeds. Most of this was done to create breeds that could do certain types of work (like hunting dogs, racing dogs, and so on). Later, these more varied breeds were mixed and bred again to create more interesting-looking dogs – to be kept as pets. But even though they look so different, Dobermanns, dachshunds, poodles and chihuahuas are all still the same species – *domestic dog*, or *Canis domesticus* – because, in theory, you could still interbreed them.

You mean a Dobermann and a chihuahua could have puppies together?

In theory, yes. Although some breeds have drifted so far apart that getting them to breed would be pretty unlikely (like these two, perhaps), that's one of the basic ways of labelling a species: its members could all have healthy offspring capable of having more offspring themselves. That's why all dog breeds are the *same* species, but cats and dogs are *different* species. There might be plenty of Rottweiler–Dobermanns about, but we won't be seeing any cogs (or dats, for that matter) any time soon.

OK, so we made dogs more different on purpose — but didn't you say dogs were easy to change too?

Yup – could be true also. Crossing two big animals doesn't automatically give you an even bigger one. And other traits – like how long the legs are, or what shape the head is – are even trickier for breeders to control. But all these traits are controlled by growth genes. And it seems that dogs may have a few simple growth genes that are passed down easily and reinforce each other strongly, giving a bigger effect when you cross-breed them.

But how do we know all this stuff?

Partly from looking at the history of dog breeding, and partly by looking directly at doggie DNA. Scientists have recently finished the Dog Genome Project, which created a map of all known dog genes and revealed every letter of the domestic dog's DNA code. Using computers to analyse the code, geneticists have found many genes related to doggie diseases and growth problems. But they've also discovered evidence of the dog's recent breeding history, and of how it relates to other animals. It's fairly obvious that dogs are related to wolves and hyenas, for example. But scientists have found that if you go further back into evolutionary history, dogs also share ancestors with raccoons, bears and even walruses!

Cool. So what will they do with all the info?

Hopefully, they'll use it to learn more about different dog breeds, how they grow and develop, and which genes cause the diseases they're prone to. This will help us develop medicines and treatments for pedigree dogs that will help them to stay healthier and live longer. It could also help identify dog genes – even ancient ones from raccoons or bears – that might help breeders produce dogs in even more shapes and sizes.

You mean like a dog with a big, stripy tail? Or huge bear-dog with massive claws and teeth?

Whoa – hold on there. It's not as easy as that.

Rubbish. I want a bear-dog *now*. Think about it, man — *instant* respect. No one would mess with me if I walked one of *those* down the street.

Perhaps. But try getting it to 'heel' if it doesn't want to. Plus you'll have to scoop some serious bear-sized dog poo . . .

Ah. Yeah. Good point.

What's the toughest animal in the world?

Probably the tardigrade or water bear – a strange insect-like animal that can survive freezing, boiling, starvation, firing into Space or even a nuclear explosion!

OK — I thought you'd say 'bears', maybe. As in 'grizzly'. But water bears? What're they?

They're weird, microscopic animals that look a bit like inflatable woodlice. With claws.

They're insects, then?

Nope. And neither are woodlice, as it happens.

They're not?

Nope. Woodlice are related to insects, as they both belong to a group called *arthropods* (which means 'jointed feet' in Greek). All arthropods have jointed legs and a hard exoskeleton, or shell, made out of a protein called chitin. So, close up, they look a bit like knights in armour.

Insects are a type of six-legged arthropod. In fact, about 95% of all arthropods are insects. The other 5% are made up of the eight-legged *arachnids* (which include spiders, scorpions, ticks and mites), the ten or twelve-legged *crustaceans* (which include crabs, lobsters, shrimp and woodlice), plus *centipedes*, *millipedes* and a few others. Tardigrades have eight legs and an exoskeleton made of chitin.

So they're arachnids, then?

Nope. They don't have proper jointed legs, so they're not even arthropods.

So what are they??

They're related to the arthropods, but so unique that they have their own group, called the *tardigrada*. These strange animals grow to just over a millimetre in length, eat tiny chunks of plant, moss and bacteria, and they live pretty much everywhere. Scientists have found over 900 species of them so far, and although many live in oceans, lakes and rivers, they also live happily on land, surrounded by a mere drop of water. They use their legs to swim, but also to move across flat surfaces with a slow, waddling bear-like walk. That walk – plus the claws – is where the names 'water bear' and 'tardigrade' come from (tardigrade means 'slow walker' in Greek).

They sound pretty feeble to me. What makes them so tough then, eh? Bet I can name loads of animals tougher than your tardi-wotsits . . .

My animals could have your animals easily.

Yeah, right!

I'm serious. They could take on any animal, in any kind of toughness test you care to think of.

All right, then. Bring it on. I'll have . . . grizzly bears. They're *well hard*.

OK. That's a good start. Grizzly bears are pretty tough. They're big, ferocious when provoked, they eat more or less anything and they can survive for up to six months without food during their winter hibernation.

Ha! You see?

... But compared to tardigrades? Wimps. Water bears can go up to *ten years* without food or water, by putting themselves into a kind of hibernation so deep they're barely alive.

All right — what about *polar* bears? Betcha your tardigrade couldn't survive in the freezing Arctic . . .

Yes, I suppose polar bears are pretty hardy too. Their thick skin and fur help them to survive in temperatures as low as −37 °C. On the other hand, tardigrades can survive temperatures lower than −200 °C. So to them the Arctic and Antarctic feel like the Bahamas. Next!

Fine. Armadillos, then. Those things that roll up into armoured balls so nothing can hurt them. Bet your tardigrade can't do *that*.

Ah, yes, armadillos. Their hard, leathery armour protects them from wolves, coyotes and even bears. But jaguars have been known to crack armadillos (and turtles) open

with their super-strong jaws. Now, I'll grant you – a jaguar's bite can generate over 300kg of pressure, so that still makes armadillos pretty tough. But drag one to the bottom of the ocean, and the crushing pressure of the water above would squash an armadillo as flat as a pancake. My super-tough mates the tardigrades, however, can survive pressures of more than 6,000kg per square centimetre, or over six times the pressure found in even the deepest ocean trench. What's more, fire an armadillo into the vacuum of Space and it would pop like a balloon. Fire a tardigrade into Space, and it'll laugh at you (well – it would if it could, I'm sure).

It could live in Space?!

Not quite. While nothing can actually *live* in Space, a tardigrade in its hibernation state could survive for a while, and revive itself later when brought back to Earth. Which is still pretty amazing.

Gahh! Right! Cockroaches!! That'll do it. I heard that cockroaches can survive a massive nuclear bomb! That they're the only things that could survive it, even! Take that!

Unfortunately, that's not quite true. Nothing could survive a direct hit from a nuclear bomb – the heat would vaporize everything up to a few miles away from where it went off – including cockroaches. But, outside that range, cockroaches would be pretty good at dealing with levels of radiation that would kill most other animals. 2,000 rads of radiation would be enough to kill a person, but cockroaches can survive up to 6,400 rads or more. Which is pretty impressive . . .

Ha-haaaaaa!! I win after all!!

. . . until you see that tardigrades can survive over 570,000 rads – making them pretty much radiation-proof.

OK, OK! Water bears are indestructible. You win.

Woo-hoo! I *rule*!

Oh, shut up . . . hey — here's a thought: if the whole world got blown up by an asteroid or something, does that mean the water bears would survive and rule over the whole planet?

Hmmmm. It's possible, I guess.

Maybe that even happened somewhere else already, and huge water-bear things are waddling around on other planets, waiting to be found . . .

Could be. Or maybe even weirder things. Perhaps one day we'll find out.

Cool! Maybe we'll find out what the toughest thing in the *Universe* is!

Then we'd just have to hope it's friendly . . .

Sci-facts: other tough guys of the animal world

A fully grown **mountain gorilla** can lift ten times its own body weight. The strongest humans can only lift about three times their weight. Overall, an average male gorilla is about as strong as six average-sized men.

For their size, **scarab beetles** are even stronger. Some can lift over 400 times their body weight, and support over 800 times their own weight on their backs.

Some **eagles** can fly carrying over four times their own weight. The best a jet airliner or cargo plane can manage is just over twice their own weight.*

Camels can lose over 25% of the water in their bodies and still survive in blistering desert heat. Most animals (including humans) die of thirst after losing just 10%.

Humans can only survive about six weeks without food. Male emperor **penguins** can manage over four months, female **polar bears** over eight months and African **lungfish** over four years!

---

* For more about the world's heaviest aeroplanes, see *How big can an aeroplane get before it's too heavy to fly?* (page 116).

Which animal swims fastest, and how fast can it go?

Difficult to say, but it could well be a tuna fish! Although sailfish, dolphins and penguins are pretty speedy too . . .

A tuna fish?! Rubbish!!

Well, it's a bit tricky to know for sure – but, believe it or not, the bluefin tuna has the highest recorded sustained swimming speed, managing a steady speed of 44mph for twenty seconds or more.

That doesn't sound so fast.

Maybe not – but take it from me, as swimmers go that's practically jet-propelled. Even the fastest human Olympic athletes have only managed about 5mph. So the bluefin tuna is about *nine times* faster than we are in the water. By comparison, cheetahs – the fastest runners on land – run just three times faster than the fastest human sprinters.

Yeah, but come on — a tuna fish? There must be something faster than that. Like a shark or something.

Actually, most sharks are fairly slow movers most of the time. They typically cruise around at three or four miles per hour – like toothy, menacing submarines – only bothering to put on short bursts of speed when they're chasing something. That said, when they do move, they can really move. Mako sharks and hammerhead sharks may be capable of speeds of up to 60mph – but only over very short distances. Similarly, some other big fish such as sailfish, wahoo and marlin may be capable of very high-speed dashes. There's one report of a sailfish that hit 68mph, which would make it the fastest fish ever recorded. But it's difficult to know for sure whether it really managed this speed or not.

What makes it so hard to find out? Can't we just follow them about with boats for a bit and time them?

Measuring underwater swimming speeds is a lot harder than clocking the sprint of, say, a cheetah or a gazelle over land. If you're on the surface, you can't see a speeding fish under the water unless it leaves a fin sticking out, so it's difficult to track and time them. Under the water, divers and submarines can observe fish swimming, but apparent distances get distorted, and the visibility is often poor. Many of the figures above (such as the 68mph sailfish) are based on estimates made by fishermen – who tend to exaggerate about how big and fast 'the one that got away' was. The only truly reliable figures are from marine biologists. They often plant radio tags or transmitters on the animals they study, and track their migrations and behaviour from the surface. It's from them that we know that the bluefin tuna migrates across the entire Pacific Ocean – and how quickly it can move when it wants to.

So what makes that tuna so special?

Basically, the bluefin is a lean, mean swimming machine. It grows up to 3.7m long, and weighs over half a tonne (680kg), most of which is lean swimming muscle. It's streamlined to reduce drag in the water and, unlike most other fish, it avoids bending its body from side to side as it swims. Instead, the bluefin holds its body straight and

rigid, and drives itself through the water like a torpedo –
using rapid, powerful beats of its crescent-shaped tail.

All right — that *is* pretty cool. But I bet a dolphin could catch one. Right?

Not in a straight race. The average bottlenose dolphin
only hits about 18–25mph when swimming hard, and has
a top speed of no more than 30mph. Not even the fastest
member of the dolphin family, the killer whale (nope – not
actually whales at all – they just got that name because of
their size) could catch a bluefin tuna going full pelt. That
said, the killer whale can power itself through the water
at 34mph, making it the fastest mammal in the ocean.

Unlike fish, killer whales and dolphins have horizontal
tails, and build up speed by beating their tails up and down,
rather than left to right. By adding a wave-like wriggle
along the length of their whole bodies, they create rolling
currents of water called shed vortexes. These push their
front fins (or *pectoral* fins) forward, while the tail beats
from behind. It's a bit like flying underwater.

Like penguins do?

Yes – penguins use the same method. And they're no slow-coaches in the water either. A gentoo penguin can 'fly' underwater like this at over 22mph for hours at a time.

Could a person swim like that to go faster? Like, sticking your arms out sideways or something?

You could, but since humans have different muscle groups in their arms, you couldn't keep it up for long. But, as a matter of fact, the US Navy is testing a kind of strap-on, underwater gliding device that lets Navy SEAL (or commando) scuba divers swim like dolphins. Two front 'wings' are strapped under the diver's chest and are linked to two more wings strapped under the diver's ankles. As the diver ripples his body, he can power silently through the water – over one and a half times faster than with scuba flippers alone.

Cool! I definitely want to try one of those. Maybe if I got really good at it, I could chase down a tuna fish with one.

OK – good luck with that . . .

What's the fastest thing on Earth?

Without a doubt, it's a particle of light. Because, as far as we know, nothing can ever go faster.

Duhhh — I didn't mean that. I meant an actual thing. Light isn't a *thing*, is it?

Yes, it is. Light is made of things too. Tiny packets of energy called photons. They don't have any actual weight (or rather, mass) but that doesn't mean they don't exist. Photons have energy, momentum and *speed*. Lots of it. They travel (surprise, surprise) at the speed of light, which is around 671 *million* mph. So photons are *definitely* the fastest things on Earth.

All right, then — what're the fastest things on Earth that actually, you know, *weigh something*? Like animals and cars and trains and planes and stuff?

Well, which one do you want first?

I dunno. Err . . . fastest animal. That's a cheetah, right?

Nope.

It isn't?

Cheetahs are pretty speedy, it's true. They can reach over 60mph at full sprint, making them the fastest land animal. But, in the air, peregrine falcons can fold their wings and go into high-speed dives that reach over 200mph – making cheetahs look like tortoises.

Wow. That *is* fast. OK — now let's do . . . the fastest train. Is it that Bullet Train in Japan?

Well, it is a Japanese train, but it's not that one. The Japanese Shinkansen or 'Bullet Train' was the fastest train when it set a new record of 275mph in 1996. But since then it has been outdone by a new class of floating, magnetic levitation (or Maglev) trains.* A Chinese Maglev train hit 267mph in November 2003, but a month later it was topped by another Maglev train on a test line in Yamanashi prefecture in Japan. That one hit 361mph. That speed may even have been beaten since, but it's pretty clear that Maglevs are currently the fastest trains in the world.

Nice. Now do cars!

The fastest car? That record still stands with the jet-powered Thrust SCC car, which hit an incredible 763mph in 1997. That's faster than the speed of sound!

Cool! Fastest plane, fastest plane!

The fastest conventional aeroplane (meaning a propeller- or jet-powered aircraft that can take off and land on its own) is the SR-71 Blackbird, which screamed though the air at 2,188mph in 1976 and still holds the record. But if we're talking about the fastest *aircraft*, then rocket planes and spacecraft launched from Earth have gone much faster.** Nine years before the Blackbird, the North American X-15 rocket plane had already reached a blistering 4,510mph in

* For more about Maglev trains, see *Will we ever ride in floating trains and buses?* (page 157).

** For more about the future of rocket flight, see *Will rockets replace aeroplanes one day?* (page 137).

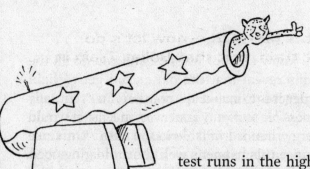

test runs in the high atmosphere. And although you might not be able to call it an aircraft (or even 'the fastest thing on Earth', since technically it's not *on* Earth any more), a Space Shuttle in orbit 'cruises' at about 17,580mph – which is so terrifyingly fast that it's difficult to imagine.

Sweeeeet. So couldn't we build even faster spaceships one day? Ones that go faster than the speed of light?

Well, we'd like to, of course. Especially since the closest star (and possibly solar system) to ours, Proxima Centauri, is over four light years, or 24 trillion miles, away. But the fastest thing we've ever built on Earth is the Voyager 1 space probe, which after whipping around the planets to pick up speed is currently (in 2008) doing over 39,000mph. At that rate, it would take over 73,000 years to reach Proxima Centauri. So we're still some way short (about 670.9 million mph, to be exact) of reaching light speed.

Quite a way to go, then . . .

Right. And most physicists say we can never reach light speed, anyway – no matter how hard we try.

Why not?

Because, if you know all your physics, and you do all the maths, the sums reveal that the closer you get to light speed, the harder it is to speed up any more. So eventually it becomes *impossible* to go any faster – or at least, it would take more energy than is available in the entire Universe to do it. And since this happens well short of light speed, we've no hope of ever actually reaching it.

Boo. That's no fun. So we'll never reach the stars, then?

Well, maybe not that way, but there may be other ways. Some physicists think we might be able to use special tunnels, or 'wormholes', in space–time to take shortcuts between stars. Or even create our own space–time tunnels by warping space–time ourselves. But again, no one has yet figured out a way of doing this without using more energy than currently exists in the Universe.

But they *might* figure it out one day, right?

Right. Anything is possible. It could be that we're wrong about space–time warping, about accelerating to light speed or even about light speed itself. Or maybe we've understood most of it, but there's a missing piece of the puzzle waiting to be discovered. And if that happens . . .

. . . then I might end up on the next flight to Proxima Centauri, after all?

Could do. You never know . . .

Is there anything hotter than the Sun?

Plenty of things – including lightning and many of the stars in the sky. In fact, as stars go, the Sun is practically lukewarm.

Lightning is hotter than the Sun?!

Well, yes and no. It depends which part of the Sun you're talking about. The Sun has many layers inside and around it, and the temperatures vary a lot between them. But if you're talking about the bit of the Sun we can see – the surface layer from which we receive sunlight – then lightning is hotter.

So, if I was totally heatproof, and I could stand on the Sun and touch it . . .

Yes . . .

. . . and I was holding a lightning bolt in the other hand, then the lightning would feel hotter?

If you were totally heatproof, then you wouldn't be able to feel either one of them.

Yeeeahhh, but come on — you know what I mean.

All right. If you *could* feel them, then yes – the lightning would be hotter.

Really?

Yup. Lightning can reach temperatures over 28,000 °C. The surface of the Sun isn't really solid like that of the

Earth (so you couldn't actually stand on it anyway, even if you *were* heatproof). But there is a boundary between the 'inside' and 'outside' of the Sun, where sunspots appear, called the *photosphere*. The temperature there ranges from 3,700 °C to 5,700 °C, making lightning about five times hotter than the 'surface' of the Sun.

But I heard that if the Sun was right next to the Earth, it would melt us.

That's true.

So if lightning hits the Earth all the time, and it's hotter than the Sun, why doesn't it melt the planet?

Partly because lightning doesn't stay that hot for very long . . . as it doesn't *exist* for very long.

Hang on — how can lightning *not exist*? You mean it's there one minute, and gone the next?

In a way, yes. What we call 'lightning' isn't really an object – it's an *event*, or a *phenomenon*. It happens when a flow of

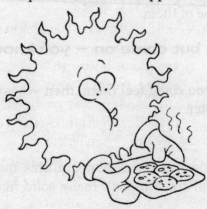

charged particles, or electrons, moves between a thunder-cloud and a target on the ground, producing a flash in the air as it goes. It works like this: in certain types of cloud an electric charge can build up as the water molecules inside move past each other.* As the charge builds up, gas atoms in the air between the cloud and the ground are temporarily stripped of their electrons, and the air turns into a super-hot plasma.

A plasma is like a fourth state of matter (beyond solids, liquids and gases) in which electrons are separated from atoms. Plasmas can reach temperatures of thousands of degrees, but as it takes so much energy to produce them they rarely stick around for long. And that's how it is with lightning. Once the plasma has formed, and the electric charge has flowed through it, the atoms and electrons clump back together again, forming normal air molecules and releasing the flash of light we usually call lightning. So the lightning only exists for as long as the plasma does. And while the plasma is very hot, it isn't there long enough (plus there's *nowhere near* enough of it) to melt the planet.

But the Sun could. Right?

Right. The Sun could *easily* melt the planet if it was close enough. It's massive, it's constant and there are parts of the Sun that are much hotter than its surface. Above the surface, super-hot plasmas form in halo-like layers around the Sun called the *chromosphere* and *corona*. Parts of the corona can reach temperatures of over 2 million °C – thousands of times hotter than lightning. And in the Sun's core, nuclear reactions drive temperatures up to 15 million °C or more.

* For more about storm clouds, see *What are clouds for?* (page 84).

Now I get it. That's why you said 'yes and no'.

Right – some bits of the Sun are five times cooler than lightning, but others are over five *hundred* times hotter.

That sounds pretty hot.

It is.

So is the Sun one of the hottest things there is?

Nope. Not by a long shot. The Sun is a large, hot star, making it incredibly hot compared to most things on Earth. But, amazingly, the Sun is pretty average as stars go. The Sun is a *yellow dwarf*. That's just one type of star, of which there are many bigger (and hotter) ones in the sky you look into every night. Yellow dwarfs are about twice as hot as *red dwarf* stars, which are smaller stars with surface temperatures of about 3,000 °C. But *blue giant* stars are many times bigger than our Sun, and are three or more times hotter. They have surface temperatures of over 18,000 °C (and remember, the surface is one of the coolest parts).

So what's the hottest type of star?

The hottest stars in the Universe are dying stars. At the end of their lives, some massive stars go out with a bang: an enormous explosion called a supernova. These reach temperatures of *billions* of degrees – hundreds of thousands of times hotter than our Sun's core – making our little star look lukewarm by comparison.

Wow. Crazy.

And I'll tell you what else is hotter than the Sun.

What?

Me. Owwwwwww. Yeah! Check out me and my bad self! I am HOT!

Riiiiight. I didn't see that coming.

Ah. Sorry.

(Sigh.)

What's the deadliest disease in the world?

The *nastiest* is probably a rare kind of fever that destroys your organs and makes your skin bleed all over. But the *deadliest* is more familiar – it's flu.

There's a disease that makes you bleed all over?! Yuck!!

Yup. Pretty nasty, eh?

What is it?

It's a disease called haemorrhagic fever, which is caused by a family of viruses called *filoviruses*. 'Filo' means 'thread' or 'string' in Latin, and the viruses get their name from the way they look under the microscope – like short loops or coils of string. Two members of this family – the Ebola and Marburg viruses – cause the disease. Thankfully, these are not very infectious (or easy to pass between people), which means they remain quite rare. Most cases so far have been in parts of Africa – largely because the monkeys that live there can carry the virus around without dying of it. Outbreaks usually happen in one village or stay within a small area, and in total only a few hundred people have died of Ebola or Marburg infections. But this is partly because it kills so quickly that it doesn't have time to spread . . .

Yikes. How do you get it, then?

Virologists (scientists that study viruses and viral diseases) still aren't sure how Ebola and Marburg are first transmitted to people. But since other filoviruses are carried by fleas and ticks on rodents and monkeys, that seems the likeliest source. It doesn't move from person to person very easily, though – you'd have to be in very close contact. And after looking at someone that has it, most people aren't keen to get too close.

Why's that? I mean – I know I'll regret this – but what does it actually do to you?

OK – you asked for it. But only read this if you have a strong stomach . . .

The virus attacks organs all over your body, including your largest single organ – your skin. The virus breeds within cells and ruptures them, causing the *symptoms* (or signs of the disease) and, eventually, death. It starts with tiredness, dizziness and a fever. Then bleeding from under the skin, from the eyes, nose, ears and mouth – pretty much anywhere and everywhere. But it isn't the bleeding that kills you. Usually, the kidneys or nervous system shut down, causing seizures, coma and death.

Yahhhh!! Grim!

Like I said – you asked.

Come on – that has to be the deadliest disease ever, right?

Well, it is very nasty, but also very rare. And in a given year it doesn't kill many people at all. Sometimes none. So it depends on what you mean by 'deadly'. Plenty of diseases are bigger killers than haemorrhagic fever.

Like what?

The top three killer diseases in the developed world are ischaemic heart disease (which causes heart attacks), cerebrovascular disease (which causes strokes) and lung infections like pneumonia. That's because most developed countries have the luxury of clean water, good sewerage systems and plenty of doctors and hospitals. In the developing world, many countries don't have these things, so different diseases are the top killers. These include malaria (which is carried by infected mosquitoes), diarrhoea-causing diseases such as cholera (which are transmitted through bacteria in unclean water), and infections that happen during childbirth. HIV/AIDS is also a huge killer – in both the developing and developed world. Although there's no cure, it does more damage in the developing world – partly because many people there have less information about how to avoid getting it.

So which one is the deadliest?

Again, that depends on what you mean by 'deadly'. Since many of these diseases are curable (or can at least be treated) you might not consider them so deadly. And while HIV/AIDS isn't curable yet, there's another incurable disease that has killed more people in one go than any other . . .

It's the plague, right?

Close. Bubonic plague, or the 'Black Death' did manage to kill millions of people during huge outbreaks in the sixth, fourteenth and seventeenth centuries. And, believe it or not, the bacterium that causes it is still around, causing several new cases of plague every year . . .

What?! Where?! Nobody told me!!

. . . but there's no need to panic, since plague is now curable with common antibiotics.

Phew!

And, besides, there's another disease that is still around, still incurable and has already topped the plague's record for most people killed in a year: flu.

What? No way! I had flu once, and I'm OK.

Well, when most people think they have flu (or, more properly, influenza), they actually just have very nasty chest colds. Real influenza knocks you off your feet for a week or more, making you feel weak, dizzy, feverish and nauseous.

But you usually get better, right?

Right. But the only reason you recover from it is because the strain of flu virus you've caught is similar to one you were exposed to earlier in the year, or the year before. Your body's immune system knows roughly what the virus looks like, so quickly figures out what it is and fights it off. But once in a while a completely new strain of flu will appear. Usually, these start off in animals (often birds or pigs) and *mutate* (or become altered) so that they can infect humans. When that happens, all hell breaks loose, as it did in 1918, when a single strain of flu infected and killed over 25 million people in one year. Compare that with 2 million people a year for the Black Death, and 3 million a year for HIV/AIDS, and you can see just how deadly flu can be.

Is that why everyone's always worried about birds with flu too?

Right. Bird flu itself isn't dangerous to humans. But, if it mutated so that it could infect people, it could lead to another outbreak like that of 1918. And nobody wants to see that.

That's it — I'm going to hide in my bedroom for the rest of the year. With all those diseases, it's *scary* out there!

I wouldn't worry too much. There are no signs of a flu or plague outbreak coming just yet. And, besides, the biggest killer of *young* people in developed countries isn't even a disease at all. It's *much* bigger than any virus or bacterium. You catch it *much* faster. And it kills on contact.

So what is it?

It's a speeding car. Traffic accidents kill over a million people per year, every year. And, unlike most diseases, they're easy enough to avoid. So just make sure you take care when you're crossing the road, and the rest of the world will take care of itself.

What's the biggest machine in the world?

That depends how you look at it. It could either be a huge atom-smasher built by scientists to explore the origins of the Universe ... or a massive, planet-sized electronic communication machine.

An atom-smasher? That sounds cool. Can you actually smash up atoms with it?

Yes, you can. Or, rather, you can use it to smash atoms and particles into each other, at close to the speed of light.*

Sounds like fun. But why would you want to do that? Just for a laugh?

You could, I suppose. But there are probably much cheaper and easier ways to have a laugh. Particularly since the machines needed to accelerate and smash the atoms together – more properly called particle accelerators – are some of the largest and most expensive machines on Earth. Physicists actually use them to explore the nature of atoms, particles and matter. They use massive amounts of energy to smash atoms into smaller and smaller pieces, then analyse the bits that fly out of the collision. By doing this, they hope to discover more about how matter (the stuff that everything is made of) works, and how it formed in the first place. If they can figure that out, they might be able to explain how the Universe came to be the way it is, where it might be headed in future and exactly how everything – from stars to planets and black holes – really works.

---

* For more about light speed, see *What's the fastest thing on Earth?* (page 247).

Quite a bit to suss out, then. So why does the machine have to be so big?

Because just like it takes a long stretch of road to accelerate a car to top speed, to get a particle to travel at nearly light speed, you need a long run-up. Very long, in fact. Even if you twist the runway around into a loop, that's still going to be one long loop.

How big?

Let me give you some idea. The Large Hadron Collider (or LHC) is the largest particle accelerator, and probably the biggest machine, in the world. It's essentially a massive ring of electromagnets buried 100m underground, on the border between France and Switzerland. In all, it's over 17 miles wide, and weighs over 38,000 tonnes. That's the same as roughly 3,800 double-decker buses.

Whoa. That is one big machine. But why did you say 'probably the biggest'?

Because it depends what you mean by 'biggest'. The LHC is almost certainly the largest single machine in the world. But only in terms of how big a space it takes up. Other machines are bigger and heavier.

Like what? Like a massive aeroplane or something?

Nope. You'd have to go bigger and heavier than that. The largest aeroplane in the world is *only* about 90m across and weighs *just* 175 tonnes (or 17.5 buses).* Impressive, but nothing on the enormous tank-tracked platform used to transport the Space Shuttle to its launch pad. Known

---

* For more about the world's biggest aeroplanes, see *How big can an aeroplane get before it's too heavy to fly?* (page 116).

as 'The Crawler', this massive tractor weighs over 2,700 tonnes (or 270 buses).

Sweet. Then that has to be the heaviest *moving* machine, right?

Not even close. A giant, mobile mine-digging machine called the Bagger 288 weighs over 45,000 tonnes, more than 7,000 tonnes heavier than even the Large Hadron Collider. The Bagger carries a huge, rotating wheel of digger buckets on the end of one crane-like arm. It measures over 300m across and 100m tall.

Brilliant!

. . . And if you count oil tankers as moving machines too, then the largest of those weighs over 750,000 tonnes (75,000 buses!) when fully loaded with oil.* In fact, depending on what you mean by 'machine', you could go way bigger than even this.

What d'you mean?

Well, a 'machine' is basically any device that uses fixed or moving parts to do work or perform a task. We build machines to do tasks we humans can't or don't want to do ourselves, or to help us to do tasks better than we could alone. A machine can be mechanical, or electronic, or both. It can just sit there and move things inside it, like a microwave or fridge. Or it might move itself around, like a car, aeroplane or oil tanker. Everything we've looked at so far falls under this definition of 'machine', but there's one we've forgotten. One that's way bigger than all the rest put together.

---

* To learn about how huge ships stay afloat, see *Why don't big metal ships just sink?* (page 112).

What's that?

The global telecommunications network. The huge planet-wide machine the whole world uses to stay in touch through phone calls, emails, Internet chat rooms and more. Add that lot up – and you've got one big machine.

But that's cheating. That's lots of different machines, not one big one. Besides — it's only a bunch of phones, computers and cables. Bet that doesn't weigh more than that massive oil tanker.

If all the parts are working together to do the same job, I think it's fair enough to call it one big machine, don't you? And you'd be surprised how much of it there is . . .

Go on, then. How big would it be?

That'll take a bit of maths, so stick with me. Right – starting with phones, there are about 1.3 billion landlines in the world, weighing about 700g each. So that's 910,000 tonnes. Then there are roughly 2.2 billion mobile phones, each weighing an average of 113g. Another 248,600 tonnes of machine right there. Computers? There are at least 600 million of those worldwide, and the average PC weighs about 50kg, adding up to another 30 million tonnes. So that's about 31.1 million tonnes of machine so far.

So far?

Right. Then you've got the system that links them all together. Even ignoring all the switchboards, routers and servers, you still need about 700 orbiting satellites to make it work. They weigh an average of 2,000kg each, so that's another 1,400 tonnes worth of chunky satellite. And while some phone and Internet signals are bounced off satellites, most actually go through huge, thick cables laid for thousands of miles across ocean floors.

Really?

Yup. There are cables right across the Atlantic Ocean between the USA and Europe, right across the Pacific Ocean from the USA to Asia and Australia, and right around the coasts of Africa and South America. In all, there are about 186,000 miles of it, which isn't far short of the distance from here to the Moon! Since these cables weigh about 5,000kg per kilometre, that's roughly 1.5 million tonnes of cable.

Crazy. So how big does that make the whole machine?

The whole thing stretches right across the Earth and about 31,665 miles out into Space either side of it (as that's how far out most of the satellites are). So, in total, the global tele-communications network 'machine' is over 3,330 miles *wide*, and weighs over *32 million tonnes*. Top that!

You didn't have to do all those sums, you know. You could've just told me it was *really* big.

Oh great. Thanks. *Now* you tell me.

Mwa ha ha ha.

Why is water wet, and is anything wetter than water?

Water is wet because of the slippery way its molecules interact, and how well they stick to things. And, believe it or not, there may be a few things just as 'wet', or even 'wetter' than water!

So what's wetter than water, and why?

Whoa. That's a lot of Ws. Try saying that five times really fast, and I'll answer the question.

What's-wetter-than-wan . . . what's-wee-ter-than-wat . . . what's-water-than-w . . .

Heh, heh.

Hey — no fair! Just tell me!!

OK – but it really all depends on what you mean by 'wet'.

How's that?

Well, in one way, 'wet' is just a name we give to something that's soaked in (or covered in) water or a water-like liquid.

OK . . .

But which is wetter – a wet blanket, or a waterfall?

Err . . . the waterfall, I suppose.

Why?

Because . . . it's more . . . watery. There's more water in it.

Right. And that's one answer to the question. If 'wet' means 'water-like', then you can't get anything more water-like than water itself, and nothing can be wetter.

Oh. Is that it, then?

Could be. But that would end this question pretty quickly, wouldn't it? So let's have a bit more fun with it, by talking about what else we mean when we say water (or another liquid) is 'wet'. And that's all to do with how liquids behave.

Don't be stupid — liquids can't behave. They can't misbehave either. They haven't got brains, so they can't decide to do anything. Duhhh.

True, but all materials and substances behave – or act – in certain ways (and without deciding to at all). A block of iron, for example, doesn't behave like water. It just sits there, happily holding its shape. It doesn't flow, drip and reshape itself to fill and fit containers like water does. And you certainly can't *wet* things with a solid block of iron.

What about if you heated it up really hot and melted it?

Right! If you melted the solid iron, it would turn into a liquid and start to flow, drip and reshape itself. But why is it that liquids behave in this 'water-like' way, but solids don't?

Err . . . dunno. Something to do with how they're made?

Yup – you've got it. It's all to do with how tightly and strongly their molecules are bound together. The molecules in a solid are locked tight into rows and columns, forming a framework a bit like a wire fence or metal cage. The cage can't bend or twist much, so the material stays in a solid lump. In liquids, the molecules are still connected but are more free to move and flow around each other. So they're more like those synchronized swimmers you see at the Olympics, who hold hands as they swim over, under and around each other – never letting go. They can form flat sheets (or pools), little spheres (or droplets) – almost any shape you can think of.

Right – now we're getting somewhere. To wet something, a liquid has to be able to flow over, around or through. As long as it's not frozen (as ice) then water can do that, quite happily. But think about this – what would happen if the water didn't actually *stick to* the material. It just flowed through it and past it, without clinging on. Would the material be wet?

You mean if *no* water stuck to it at all? Not even a drop?

Right. Not even a drop.

Err . . . then . . . no. I s'pose not. It'd be dry.

Right. So it's not enough for a liquid to flow in order to wet something – it also has to stick to the surface of a material, or soak into it and stick inside. And that stickiness is down to something else – something called *surface tension*. This is the force that holds water droplets together as the water molecules stick to themselves in a ball. But surface tension can also form bridging layers across liquid surfaces. (This is why those insects you see skating across the surface of ponds don't fall through into the water – they're skating on this 'molecule bridge' at the surface.) And, within a material, it forms bridges of water molecules between the fibres of your shirt, hair, trunks or whatever. Water has a very high surface tension (as liquids go) and this helps it stick to materials and keep them soggy.

So what happens when they dry out?

Well, if you leave them for long enough, the water molecules will absorb heat from the air around them and evaporate – turning the liquid bridges into a gas (water vapour) that floats away. You can speed this up, of course, by heating them (with, say, a tumble-dryer or hair dryer). Shaking, rubbing or wringing out your clothes will also speed things up because when you do this the water molecules become unstuck from the material and stick to themselves instead, forming droplets. These droplets fly off and eventually evaporate too.

Hang on — if water's so great at flowing around and sticking to things to make them wet, then how can anything be wetter than water?

Because some liquids – like alcohols and chemical solvents – can flow, drip and splash just like water, but they have slightly lower surface tensions. This means their molecules are less likely to cling to themselves in droplets, and more likely to cling to other materials instead, making the materials even wetter. (Not forming so many big droplets also lets them get into smaller spaces and cracks within materials and fibres, making them very useful for cleaning.) So, in a way, these other liquids are 'wetter' than water!

Weird. Next you'll be telling me there's something drier than a bone.

Actually, your bones do contain quite a bit of water, so there are quite a few things . . .

Fine. Harder than a nail, then.

That depends what the nail is made of. Iron ones? Steel? And then of course, you could melt them . . .

Hmmm. I need some tougher questions . . .

Afterword

I hope you've enjoyed this book, and that maybe it has made you want to find out more about science, technology and how the world works. Science plays such an important role in today's world that everyone needs to know at least a bit about it to understand what's going on.

But, more than that, learning about science can be so much fun, if you go about it in the right way. All you have to do is keep asking questions, and science can open up doorways to whole new worlds of understanding and fun. Science isn't just mine – it's yours. So take it, use it and play with it. Trust me – you'll be glad you did.

Here's a good question to think about:

> You got a question from:
> **Name:** Alexander
> **Question:** What will happen if there is no science?

Without science, there would be no more machines, no more technology, no more new medicines, no more exploration of Space and no hope of saving the environment here on Earth. Science keeps the world moving forwards. We should thank it for that.

And finally:

You got a question from:
Name: Mia
Question: How important is school and how big does a platypus get??

I'd say it's very important. School sets you up for a lifetime of learning and, though it might seem hard at times, the things you learn and the friends you make can keep you smiling for years after you leave. So keep at it.

Oh, and it's about 60cm long for a male, 50cm for a female.

Thanks,

Glenn

Appendix

Questions you'll probably never need the answers to

Lots of you surprised me by visiting the Ask Glenn web page and leaving questions not about science, not about technology, but about . . . well . . . me. Although I didn't ask for these, it seems rude not to answer at least a few of them somewhere. So I'll leave you with a small selection. Cheers.

You got a question from:
Name: Mitchell
Question: Sup you gangsta wats happenin

'Sup. Not much, Dog.

You got a question from:
Name: Jorge
Question: What is your name?

Err . . . it's Glenn. Says so on the web page, I think.

You got a question from:
Name: jjjjjjjjjjjjjjjjjjjjjjjjjjjjjjjjj
Question: How old are you

Thirty-two right now, but maybe older by the time you read this.

You got a question from:
Name: Lauren
Question: What do you like to do?

Read books, watch movies, play guitar, play sports, go out, have fun. All the usual stuff, really.

You got a question from:
Name: Natalia
Question: What is your favourite colour?

Blue.

You got a question from:
Name: Anisa
Question: Do you like pets?

Yes. I have a very large and angry cat who sits with me while I write, and scowls at me cos I'm ignoring her.

You got a question from:
Name: Chloe maynard
Question: Can you hop like a frog

Yes. But not very well.

You got a question from:
Name: Jamie
Question: R u ok and do u like science

Yeah, fine, thanks. And yes – I do.

You got a question from:
Name: Philip
Question: Are you albert einstein

Err . . . no. Albert Einstein is Albert Einstein. And he's dead. Sorry.

You got a question from:
Name: Matthew
Question: Have you ever had a girlfriend? Do you like cheese as much as I do? Do you have hairy armpits? Do you have two butt chins on your ear? Do you like rabbits? Do you have a lot of money? Want to play hangman? Will you say goodbye?

Yes, dunno, yes, no, yes, no, not just now, and yes. Goodbye.

You got a question from:
Name: Clark
Question: Hey glenn wassup im still needing my project to be finished so if you could get working on it . . .

Index

Why is SNOT green?

The First Science Museum Question and Answer Book

Glenn Murphy

Why is snot green? Do rabbits fart? What is space made of? Where does all the water go at low tide? Can animals talk? What are scabs for? Will computers ever be cleverer than people?

Discover the answers to these and an awful lot of other brilliant questions frequently asked at the Science Museum in this wonderfully funny and informative book.

A selected list of titles available from Macmillan Children's Books

The prices shown below are correct at the time of going to press. However, Macmillan Publishers reserves the right to show new retail prices on covers, which may differ from those previously advertised.

All Pan Macmillan titles can be ordered from our website, www.panmacmillan.com, or from your local bookshop and are also available by post from:

Bookpost, PO Box 29, Douglas, Isle of Man IM99 1BQ

Credit cards accepted. For details:
Telephone: 01624 677237
Fax: 01624 670923
Email: bookshop@enterprise.net
www.bookpost.co.uk

Free postage and packing in the United Kingdom